APOCALYSPE AVERTED

WHY THERE WAS NO NEED TO FRET

PETER C ALVET

createspace – an amazon company

For the Grand kids

"I've always appreciated your perspective Peter. Your level-headed voice adds to the necessary discussion. You've brought a much needed, even if it is biased, dialogue to the national conversation on politics."

Donna Perdue, Florida

"Your blog (or so it appears to me) is an entreaty to all rational, forward-thinking Americans to see things from a perspective that focuses on the larger picture and holds governance to its stated purpose: doing the most good for the most people. I'm honored to be offered the chance to be included in a rational discourse on what we're getting right and where we still need work."

Dawn Brawley, South Carolina

"Even in defeat, the GOP spin machine nearly convinced me that Obama's election was, somehow, a mistake…not just unlikely, but impossible. The reason such folks have such difficulty admitting defeat is "Truthiness." They've been lying and dissembling for so long….and and so well… they have come to believe in their own distorted, destructive reality…"

James Sandel, Massachusetts

"I like how you think. Keep it up. Makes me think outside the box."

Eve Buckle Dorf, California.

Introduction

The birth of this blog came about over a year ago when I decided to participate in the upcoming election in a significant way. Since I predicted back in September 2011 that Mitt Romney was going to be the Republican nominee, I selected his signature statement, "Corporations are People" as the name of my blog. Not only did this phrase capture the essence of what Romney stood for, it also captured what the tenor of the election was going to be.

Thanks to the *Citizen's United* Supreme Court decision essentially giving *Carte Blanche* to the monied interests to spend unlimited cash on political campaigns the term "Corporations are People" seemed to encapsulate this new experiment in electoral politics. The addition of a question mark at the end was my wife Gisela's idea which indeed reflects my attitude towards this new enterprise.

One of the many lessons we learned from this extravagant campaign is that the private sector is not very good at using funds in pursuit of public goals. We are lucky that the billionaires who gave immense sums of money in order to defeat who they perceive as their arch-enemy did not have access to public funds. It is one thing to be reckless with your own money – quite another to be reckless with the people's money. So the promoters of government frugality spent more money than an entire aircraft carrier of drunken sailors in a futile, self-defeating effort to unseat the radical menace that they think is the President of the United States. Had they supported the modest increase in taxation that the expiration of the Bush tax cuts represent, they would have saved themselves a bundle, not to mention extreme embarrassment.

The enclosed chapters are mostly about the election but since I don't have the burden of reporting to a tyrannical editor with all the accompanying rules and deadlines, the topics tend to be somewhat capricious and haphazard. There is a chronology of sorts since each chapter has a date attached to it. I leave in the reader's capable hands to determine whether I was prescient or off the mark.

I suppose a little of both.

Bristol, Rhode Island, March 1, 2013

Contents

Introduction - 7

Reflections on 9/11 - 12

Bachmann Goes Over the Cliff - 15

That's the Way They are in Texas - 18

Obama's Revenge - 21

Republican Class Warfare - 24

The New Republican Party - 28

Christie Recognizes the Obvious - 32

Cain Knocks Himself Out - 35

Tea Party Sells Out - 37

Bigots in Government - 40

The Rumble in Vegas - 43

Huntsman: The Forgotten Candidate - 47

The Most Dangerous Man in America - 50

The Price of Prejudice - 54

The Norquist Era Slowly Ending - 57

Right Wing in Retreat - 60

Republican Darwinism - 63

Sad State of Foreign Affairs - 66

An Unlikely Hero - 69

A Modest Proposal - 72

Dirty Little Secret - 76

Newt's Woman Problem - 83

Newtonian Justice - 86

Rheumatic Republicans - 90

Who Cares About Iowa? - 96

Ron Paul's Excellent Adventure - 101

The Real Freedom Fighter - 107

Santorum Flunks Leadership - 110

The Politics of Misinformation - 113

Deep Into the Weeds - 117

Moscow's Blunder - 138

Religion and Politics - 141

The President's Budget - 145

The Last Gasps of Dinosaurs - 152

Franklin Graham Crosses the Line - 157

Santorum Flunks Again - 161

Rush Must Go! - 166

Religion and Civilization - 172

Exploiting Fear for Profit - 177

Religion and Civilization Part II - 181

"Stand Your Ground" - 187

The Good Wife - 191

The Paul Ryan Paradox - 195

The Real Job Creators - 200

The Reverend Wright Digression - 206

The Lessons of the Walker Recall - 212

The Great Gas Gambit - 216

The Dysfunction Myth - 219

Malicious Kook Power - 222

The Ugly American - 226

America's decline? - 230

Ryan's Medicare Problem - 234

Dirty Harry Meets Harvey - 239

Bopp 'til you Drop - 245

Voodoo Two - 249

Mitt's Pyrrhic Victory - 254

Romney's Military-Industrial Complex - 259

Joe Scores a KO - 264

The President Gets His Groove Back - 269

The Closer Versus the Strategist - 272

The Next Four Years - 278

Apocalypse Averted - 282

Reflections on 9/11

The war in Iraq was indeed an ill-conceived incursion. Not that Saddam was an "innocent". Certainly he was not. It was, however, an admission on the part of the Bush administration that action, even rash action was better than no action.

The war in Afghanistan was unsatisfying in that when Bin Laden eluded the allies, it became an amorphous situation - we were fighting a culture rather than an enemy. Much as we all thought the Taliban were awful, they were no more awful than so many other tribal groups around the world with their less than modern and less than enlightened attitudes. But they did not have a leader that could rise to the level of "evil", which is what Bush so desperately wanted.

Now Saddam Hussein, he was an easy embodiment of evil. No matter that he had nothing to do with 9/11. He was to be the stand in for all the bad guys who attacked America. He had it all. If Hollywood were to design a "bad guy" he would be it. A ruthless dictator, with scum for sons. A guy who committed mass murder, who was a sexual pervert, was hated by his own people. He was the perfect foil for America so he was picked as the man the country could galvanize against.

But in spite of all Bush's machinations, the American people have a sense of fairness about them. They were ready to embark on a crusade at the beginning until some of them started to feel manipulated. Was this the guy who was really guilty? And it became increasingly clear that Hussein was the victim of a type of lynch mob, a phenomenon Americans know all too well. Get the handiest guilty looking guy and string him up the nearest tree, because someone has to pay for all this hurt.

And when Americans found out we hanged the wrong guy, they turned on the President who duped them. Enter Obama, a real sheriff, who decided that the law was more important than the feel good atmosphere of the previous administration. He calmly set about reviewing the facts, put together a posse and went after the real culprit and shot him in the head, just like John Wayne would have done. Rough justice. The kind of justice we saw in the movies when we were kids.

And Obama, the multi-lateralist whose instincts are always to seek partners didn't ask for permission to shoot the real bad guy. He just did it because in the end he knew nobody would complain. The creep deserved it. Good riddance. Even the Arab Street was silent.

The Pakistanis screamed but they were caught with their collective pants down and were embarrassed. Embarrassed because Bin Laden was living under their noses, and their American allies didn't trust them.

Had Bush pulled this off within a year of 9/11 and never gone into Iraq as it wouldn't have been necessary he would still be a hero. But because he failed at getting the real bad guy he felt the need to manufacture one. So what was a relatively simple task turned into a very costly saga.

The irony is that Bush, being from Texas should have been more familiar with the Western movie genre and should have realized that you always get the bad guy if you want to be the hero. He failed cowboy 101.

September 12, 2011

Bachmann Goes Over the Cliff

It's official. Michele Bachmann will not be the GOP's candidate for President. Her latest gaffe is not really a mistake. It is a monstrous lie:

"She told me that her little daughter took that vaccine, that injection, and she suffered from mental retardation thereafter," Bachmann said. "There is no second chance for these little girls if there is any dangerous consequences to their bodies."

This little quote will sink her candidacy in that unless the woman's daughter in question has the only case of mental retardation due to a legal vaccine. Most likely, Bachmann is deliberately lying in a desperate move to save her relevancy in the quest for the Republican nomination. Bachmann is accustomed to telling whoppers to her adoring fans in closed venues but doesn't seem to realize that in an open and democratic society everything is subject to scrutiny. She will, of course, blame the "lamestreet" media for quoting her incorrectly or some other such excuse, but it will be very hard for her to confront the facts since it is inevitable that we will find out who this alleged woman is, what she really said, and exactly the total circumstances of her daughter..

It is too early to speculate on exactly what, if anything, took place, but it is highly improbable that a young girl became mentally retarded as a result of a vaccine. If this were indeed the case, it would be a huge story and the medical community would have to seriously re-examine the vaccination programs that are in existence.

But since Michele Bachmann is making these allegations, very few people are taking her very seriously but they should. If Bachmann or any other politician is allowed to get away with such a monstrous lie, then it will call into question anything any public figure says, who swore an oath to defend the Constitution and thereby protect the well-being of American citizens.

There are, unfortunately, fringe candidates who behave more like cult leaders than public servants who are now entering the mainstream political discourse. We have seen a debasing of the body politic with trash talk that gets covered by the media as legitimate points of view. The "birther" movement in another era would have been dismissed as crazy talk. Can you imagine Walter Cronkite giving air time to crazies like that? But the advent of the 24 hour a day news channels there is a need for as much "news" as possible so otherwise ridiculous statements would never see the light of day or given any credibility.

Michele Bachmann has finally stepped over the line with her vaccine allegations because it is one thing to allege the President of the United States is not really an American, an absurd statement but not really dangerous to the citizenry, but it is quite a different matter to deliberately put children's health in jeopardy in order to score political points.

Americans will not forgive Bachmann and she will sink to the bottom of the Republican group. She only has one course of action – apologize to the American people and drop out of the race. If she does she might be able to salvage her seat in Congress.

September 14, 2011

That's the Way
They are in Texas

"Texas Gov. Rick Perry likes to tell Washington to stop meddling in state affairs. He vocally opposed the Obama administration's 2009 stimulus program to spur the economy and assist cash-strapped states. Perry also likes to trumpet that his state balanced its budget in 2009, while keeping billions in its rainy day fund. But he couldn't have done that without a lot of help from ... guess where? Washington. Turns out Texas was the state that depended the most on those very stimulus funds to plug nearly 97% of its shortfall for fiscal 2010, according to the National Conference of State Legislatures."

This quote from Matthew Yglesias pretty much sums up Governor Perry's fiscal hypocrisy. This is the man Republicans think is going to save our economy and our fiscal crisis? If this did not have serious ramifications for our country it would be very funny. So far, only the comedians are making a big deal about Perry's hypocrisy. It is pathetic that we have to rely on the likes of Jon Stewart for the truth. As an erstwhile college student once explained: "We watch the news for facts, we watch Jon Stewart for the truth."

And the truth is in very short supply. It has become a luxury commodity - an exception to the rule. And it is not just factual information like when Senator Jon Kyle was caught in a flagrant lie about Planned Parenthood, his spokesman having the nerve to state that the Senator's whopper was "not intended as a factual statement."

Falsehoods are now permitted to define people's personality. Rick Perry's Christian religiosity is a case in point. He makes a point of very publicly and loudly proclaiming his faith stooping to the obligatory humility tinged with self-flagellation. When defending himself against the demagogic Bachmann, he went as far as telling the world that even though he erred in imposing vaccinations on young girls in Texas schools, he did so because he always will err on the side of life. A seeming principled stand that incidentally fell flat with the Tea Party crowd. Bachmann's syrupy defense of little girls got the lion's share of the applause. But the biggest applause line was reserved for the announcement of 254 executions under Perry's administration. Even the unflappable Wolf Blitzer seemed a bit taken aback.

And nobody in the crowd, including most pundits seemed to notice the disconnect between Perry's professed Christianity and the glee he had in taking credit for all those executions. I suppose that most of the crowd, being Christian and pro-death penalty didn't find anything strange that a follower of the Prince of Peace was so sanguine. To loosely quote Texas singer Ry Cooder, 'That's the way they are in Texas" as if that is some sort of excuse.

And doesn't that explain so much of our contemporary political discourse? Obama, who is perceived as a decent man gets flack when he does anything that is sensed immoral or even amoral. But politicians like Bachmann, Palin, Perry, and so many others can lie through their teeth because we all accept "that's how they are." It's like giving uncle Joe a pass when he molests the young girls at the family reunion. There he goes again. How cute.

Well, there is nothing cute (including uncle Joe) when politicians are found to be liars, hypocrites, and otherwise immoral people. These are people who are role models and who are representatives of our country around the world. If we allow people of low moral character to represent us, then what does that say about us?

September 15, 2011

Obama's Revenge

The pundits are wrong. The conservatives overreached. The liberals whined prematurely.

Obama is not a wimp. Bush talked tough about Bin Laden, but let him slip by. Obama spoke softly about terrorism but hunted Bin Laden down and shot him in the head and dumped him in the ocean.

Beware of soft-spoken leaders. They are not to be trifled with. They will bite you in the butt every time, especially when you're not expecting it.

The Republicans made a huge mistake by not cooperating with Obama when they had the chance. They could have had a huge influence on major legislation. They would be partners in a successful program to revitalize America, but they chose to be obstructionists. And the worst kind of resisters. Not resisters to get a better deal for themselves but rather resisters just to thwart the President, to bring his numbers down. And by and large they succeeded. They drove Obama's numbers down, but at great cost to the Congress itself which is at a historical low. The Republicans are in fact the political equivalent of suicide bombers – they know how to inflict damage but the greatest damage is to themselves.

And Obama is going to mop the floor with them. Not since Truman has there been such an opportunity for a President to run against a no-nothing do-nothing Congress. And they are still convinced they can push this President around, much the same way the Republicans of old thought they could push Truman around because he had mistakenly acquired the reputation of being a wimp, thanks to General Douglas MacArthur, when the President refused to go along with his desire to invade China. They forgot that this was the only leader in history that dropped not one, but two atomic bombs in war, bringing an end to World War II.

Likewise, the steely calm Obama was the commander-in chief that not only killed Bin Laden but dealt decisively with Somali pirates with surgical precision and got rid of the dictator Gaddafi without losing one soldier in battle at a fraction of the cost of ridding the planet of Saddam Hussein. That is some wimp. (even Rush Limbaugh felt sorry for the pirates)

And the Republicans who have the most miniscule of support nationwide are now going to face the wrath of Obama who is fed up with their shenanigans. He is going to put the screws to the Republicans, first with his Jobs plan and now with his tax the millionaires plan, two policy points the vast majority of Americans support. This will inevitably put the Republicans in the uncomfortable position of being against jobs for Americans and protecting millionaires which the Republican candidate whether he be Rick Perry or Mitt Romney will have to run on.

This is not to say the campaign will be easy for the President, because there is real frustration in the country due to the sluggish rate of economic recovery. But when faced with the choice between a President who is fighting for them and a Party whose idea of economic recovery is George W. Bush's tax breaks for millionaires, it will be a Truman type turnaround all over again.

September 19, 2011

Republican Class Warfare

So you probably thought "Class Warfare" was a Democrat versus Republican thing. Labor versus management. Rich versus poor. Elites versus the masses. Marxists versus Capitalists. After all, it was Karl Marx who practically invented the term. "Workers of the World, unite! You have nothing to lose but your chains!" That's the way the narrative goes. Democrats represent ordinary people. Republicans represent fat cats.

As soon as President Obama announced his "tax millionaires" plan the predicable and scripted protests came from concerned Republicans. "Class Warfare!" they howled, adding yet another not so subtle reference to Obama's alleged Marxist tendencies. Pointing out his supposed disdain for the entrepreneurial class and fat cats in general. It wasn't enough that he bailed out most of the Wall Street bankers and their sorry asses. It wasn't enough that he bailed out mega corporation GM, Government Motors as they disparagingly decried. No, this President has it in for the business community because he doesn't understand capitalism, he was too busy studying how to bring down America when he went to Harvard, that bastion of commies and perverts. It's a nice fantasy. And for those folks who don't much care for science or facts, it is comforting to know that their disdain for this President has nothing to do with his race. It is he who hates us and what we stand for.

Well there is another reality out there. Because Republicans don't just play the class card against Democrats. They play it against each other. The clash between Rick Perry and Mitt Romney is being played out on a class warfare field. Since they differ very slightly on policy, the main distinction of the two is class. Perry, being a proud member of the class of under-achievers is quick to point out he didn't do so well in school. At least George W. got his "C's" at Harvard. Perry flunked courses at Texas A&M, not exactly known for academic excellence. George W. was a beneficiary of affirmative action, the kind that existed since Colonial days. If Dad was well-off, you got in, no questions asked. Perry likes to boast that his Dad never got anything handed to him, nor did he. He had to fight for everything he got, which wasn't too much. He wanted to be a vet, but couldn't make the grade and settled for politics where having a little gumption gets you a long way. There's a sucker born every minute as the saying goes. And in classic Elmer Gantry fashion he found religion along the way.

Romney, on the other hand is the classic "Rockefeller Republican", pro-business because these are the only people he socializes with, but otherwise fairly liberal until he has to run in a Republican primary where people question science. Romney knew science when he was at Harvard, but has conveniently forgotten all the knowledge his parents insured that he got. Because in order to obtain the new conservative vote you must at least pretend you are a know-nothing. So the suave and debonaire Romney has to pretend he is one of the unwashed masses. He will be guzzling beer and munching on bratwurst in no time at all. No quiche for Mr. Romney. Maybe an extravagant dinner with Mr. Trump because nobody ever accused Trump of having any class.

But make no mistake. The Perry-Romney fight is all about class warfare. And in this battlefield Perry has the edge. Nobody is going to mistake Perry for an elitist. Nobody is going to mistake Perry for an intellectual, someone who actually knows things. No-sirree Bob, Perry is all gut and no brain, and proud of it. He didn't get to where he is today by being soft, or turning down any deal, no matter how shady. Ethics? That's for losers. And they just don't put much stock in ethics at Texas A&M. A man's gotta do what a man's gotta do. And Perry did what he had to do to make it. Maybe cutting a few corners here and there, but when you're from the wrong side of the tracks, people forgive you. But Romney, he was raised to respect his elders and play by the rules. There are socially acceptable ways to rip people off. Like buying up companies and dumping excess employees. That's how Romney will grow the economy. Think of all the thousands of jobs that aren't really necessary. And we all know that unions just get in the way with their insistence on a living wage and safety in the workplace. Like who needs OSHA, or the EPA? Just bothersome bureaucrats who just get in the way of bigger profits. A Romney world is one where the corporate CEO's are finally free at last. Think of Romney as the Martin Luther King Jr. of big business. So here we have it - the dual of titans. In one corner, the pugnacious Perry, and in the other corner the rapacious Romney. May the less scrupulous man win.

September 21, 2011

The New Republican Party

When I was a kid I remember the President of the United States as a kindly old gentleman. I was told he was the Supreme Allied Commander that defeated Hitler. That in itself was impressive. But as President he was very relaxed and seemed like he played a lot of golf. Although a life-long Republican, his views were moderate, and the country was thriving. The two things I remember about Dwight Eisenhower was that he spent a fortune building one of the most important infrastructure projects in our nation's history, the interstate highway system, and his iconic parting shot when he left the Presidency. It is worth remembering his exact words:

> In the councils of government, we must guard against the acquisition of unwarranted influence, whether sought or unsought, by the military-industrial complex. The potential for the disastrous rise of misplaced power exists and will persist. We must never let the weight of this combination endanger our liberties or democratic processes. We should take nothing for granted. Only an alert and knowledgeable citizenry can compel the proper meshing of the huge industrial and military machinery of defense with our peaceful methods and goals, so that security and liberty may prosper together.

But that is not all he did. He founded NASA, another huge government project. He expanded the scope of Social Security. He sent Federal troops to enforce anti-segregation laws, and was instrumental in ridding the country of right-wing extremist Joe McCarthy. The Party always had its share of extremists. Joe McCarthy comes to mind but he left in disgrace. The John Birch Society was vilified by none other than super-conservative William F. Buckley who did not want to be associated with fanatics who were so distrustful of government they concocted a menacing conspiracy out of public water fluoridation. But these extreme folks were always considered, even by Republicans as kooks, and marginal to our political discourse. Nixon started the well-meaning Bilingual Education program, and engaged direct talks with the dreaded communist Chinese. Ronald Reagan worked with *über*-liberal Speaker Tip O'Neil to save Social Security for a generation and raised taxes when he felt the need to. It is doubtful than Eisenhower, Nixon, and even Reagan could obtain the Republican nomination these days. It seems that the kooks have taken over what was proudly called the Grand Old Party. The current talk is that the base of the party is looking for somebody who is as extreme as possible but also electable, an oxymoron if I ever heard one. They had two perfectly good candidates who fit the electable bill, Tim Pawlenty, who was essentially hounded out of the race, and Jon Hunstman, a thinking man's candidate who is near the bottom in popularity because he believes in science.

But the Republicans are like a suitor who cannot make up his mind who he wants to marry. It is understandable that the flip-flopping Romney has minimal appeal, but Rick Perry is what they wanted. He would be a disaster as President but he fits the exact bill of what the Tea Party wants. He is George W. Bush with less brains. Bachmann was the darling for a while but the sexism finally kicked in and she's apparently not qualified any more. Herman Cain got a bump in Florida, but he is clearly over his head. He may know how to run a company, but running a government is not like running a company. Ron Paul is a nice man, a sincere man with a loyal fan base but has really kooky ideas like bringing back the gold standard. He may be too nice a guy for the job. And the latest darling of the week is Chris Christie whose main appeal to the Tea Party types is his bullying style. Maybe that works in New Jersey, but Congress will make mince meat out of him. The once proud GOP, party of Abraham Lincoln has clearly gone to the dogs. It has produced some real statesmen in the past, men who were not afraid to stand for things that might not be popular with the most extreme elements of their party. But today the few leaders they have, are vilified and only people who slavishly follow the worst instincts of humanity have a chance, and even those, like Bachmann and Perry get nitpicked to death. Nothing seems to please this group of intransigent voters. Compromise, which is the lifeblood of politics, is a dirty word for them. And some of this is infecting the Democrats as well as Obama gets nitpicked by his own supporters. But all is not lost. We are still a vibrant nation. We are still a reasonable nation. We are still a generous nation. Unfortunately it is the unreasonable people who get all the attention. Reasonableness is not sexy as Obama has learned the hard way. But ultimately, reason will prevail.

September 28, 2011

Christie Recognizes the Obvious

Don't be fooled by Chris Christie's modest demeanor. The Governor of New Jersey is a hungry ambitious man who would jump at the chance at being President of the United States. He has known for quite some time that beating President Obama is not going to be as easy as the pundit class makes it out to be. Of course, if you ask people, even Obama supporters, if they are as enthusiastic as they were in 2008 in supporting the President they will obviously say no. How would it be possible to top the almost frenetic enthusiasm surrounding the election of Barack Obama, four years later? Especially when he has been repeatedly frustrated by Republican obstruction and was forced into unpopular compromises. The question should not be are you more enthusiastic, or even are you as enthusiastic. The question is do you think Obama in the White House is better for the country than going back to the policies that put us in this mess in the first place.

If you ask people if they prefer a second Obama term rather than a return to the same policies (more or less) of the George W. Bush administration, most people would prefer the former over the latter. This is precisely the calculation that Christie made. Why did it take him so long to make up his mind? Hint: it wasn't because Christie is a namby-pamby person incapable of making up his mind. This is an extremely focused and direct individual almost devoid of affectation. A plain-speaking and blunt guy who doesn't spend a lot of time agonizing over decisions. So clearly Christie was doing something else. He admits his family was supportive so he didn't use them as an excuse, so what else is there? His official explanation is the ultimate politically correct statement. He did it for New Jersey, his home state that he loves so much. But he knew that all along, so why did he have to contemplate it some more? Imagine someone suggesting you should leave your wife and then spending weeks thinking about it and then coming to the conclusion that you love her after all. How insulting is that? No, Mr. Christie put his advisers and talent to work, analyzing the path to the White House and kept coming up short. His path to the nomination was easy enough. Romney is the perpetual Plan B and Perry is just not ready for prime time so Christie was the man of the hour.

Ironically, the man with the best chance of beating Obama is neither one of them but Herman Cain. Unfortunately for Cain, he is in the wrong Party. After all, there is a reason why Black people support Democrats by over 90%. Cain is in a virtual tie with Perry and Romney but the pundits are still behaving as if this was a two way race. Cain is going to find out the hard way that there are too many racists in the conservative community to give him a real shot. But Christie's shot against Obama is much more problematic. The numbers just don't add up, according to Christie's advisers and you can believe they looked at every possible scenario. Or else, what the hell were they doing all that time? Playing cards with billionaire donors? I doubt it. Christie is a rather simple nuts and bolts politician which is the basis of his appeal. As he so eloquently stated, "Now is not my time."

That says it all.

October 4, 2011

Cain Knocks Himself Out

In response to a question about the demonstrations on Wall Street, Herman Cain said:

"Don't blame Wall Street, don't blame the big banks, if you don't have a job and you're not rich, blame yourself!"

Herman Cain just demonstrated why he won't be the next President of the United States. He doesn't have to wait for the Republican Party to reject him. He has nullified his chances of beating Barack Obama. In his own words, he only has himself to blame.

It is really too bad because Cain was one of the few candidates in the Republican field who generally does not resort to "crazy talk" to endear himself with the Tea Party crowd. His statement blaming the unemployed for their lack of employment will score points with the ultras but will not go over very big with the vast majority of American voters. Romney, the much more seasoned politician had the good sense not to touch the Wall Street protesters. That shows he has been around the block a few times and is not about to alienate the millions of people affected by unemployment.

Ironically, Cain's insensitivity towards out of work folks will probably go over well with his Party whose disdain for ordinary folks is legendary. But unfortunately for Cain, most Americans are indeed ordinary folks and probably know people who are unemployed through no fault of their own and for no lack of trying.

The Republican Party has historically favored "winners" over "losers" which is a caricature of American culture. I say caricature because there is some truth to the proposition that Americans celebrate winners. A good part of the American Dream is striving for achievement, and the success of the Republican Party is in great measure attributable to exploiting the ordinary person's desire to be doing well. Which is why Republicans worship "job creators" as the paragons of American virtue. Whereas there is nothing wrong with aspiring to succeed, it is not quite the same as despising those who have not.

Americans love winners, but they also root for the underdog. If this sounds like a contradiction it is really not. George W. Bush accepted this when he called himself a "compassionate conservative" trying to capture the essence of America. Americans are indeed compassionate and generous to a fault which is why they have little patience for the strong stepping all over the weak. Herman Cain will learn this lesson eventually. It is the duty of the strong to look out for the weak, or at least not beat them when they're down. Herman Cain is the latest Republican to take himself out of the race by not understanding the essence of America and has only himself to blame.

October 6, 2011

Tea Party Sells Out

After all the gnashing of teeth from the Tea Party whose members keep saying they won't quit until they are satisfied with a "patriotic" American for President, the Republican Party is slowly settling for the ultimate empty suit. Mitt Romney is the quintessential Hollywood Presidential candidate. Impeccably coiffed with the touch of gray at the temples, he looks and sounds like a B picture actor. Kind of like a poor man's Ronald Reagan. At least Reagan was an actual actor playing a politician, not a politician playing an actor.

Romney is everything the Tea Party says they hate. He gives phony politicians a bad name. He is on both sides of practically every issue. He's pro-choice and pro-life. He's for medical insurance mandates and against insurance mandates. He's pro bailouts when Republicans are in charge, against bailouts when Democrats are in charge.

His economic "manifesto" reads like soggy wet noodles. It is essentially a lukewarm rehash of George W. Bush policies. His justification for running is based on the Wall Street canard that the President is "anti-business" and "anti-jobs".

He's for energy independence but asserts that green technology doesn't produce enough jobs. He's for jobs but his record as a job creator in the private sector is to "restructure" companies so they can do better with less people. Mr. Efficiency. Which is great for the bottom line but doesn't create jobs.

As governor of Massachusetts, his only claim for political leadership, he ranked 47th out of 50 in job creation.

Government is indeed a bitch. Those pesky legislators don't always do what you want them to do. Just ask Obama. He can tell you how cooperative legislators can be.

Mitt decries the government bond downgrade under Obama without mentioning the downgrade was a direct result of Tea Party intransigence and the total failure of leadership on the part of the Speaker of the House, Mr. John Boehner. Mitt expects Obama to reign in recalcitrant Republicans but has no problem with the Republican leader who is incapable of reigning in members of his own party.

It will be interesting to see how Romney will juxtapose himself to Obama in the campaign as it is increasingly clear he will be the default Republican candidate since the vociferous Tea Party folks have all of sudden lost their voice. Must be the flu season.

The only part of his shtick where Romney decided to act strong, (emphasis on the acting part) is against China, that wonderful whipping boy that genius Donald Trump trumpeted. It is quite safe to lob fake grenades at the Chinese who fortunately are smart enough to realize the theatrical nature of American politics. If Romney got to be President he would come to the astounding realization that a real trade war with China would not be in our interest and the whole China talk would conveniently be forgotten.

Mitt Romney is the embodiment of an establishment politician who will say anything to get elected. He is the epitome of the corruption of insider Washington. He is everything the Tea Party says they are against. Either the Tea Party is irrelevant to American politics or they are not what they say they are.

Hard to tell the difference.

October 12, 2011

Bigots in Government

Sometimes a small example illustrates a larger point. Republican State Rep. Al Baldasaro is a case in point. It is worth remembering that a soldier who was serving in the field, Steven Hill, who is openly gay asked the Republican candidates for President what their stand on gays serving in the military was and would they re-institute the "Don't Ask Don't Tell" policy. Only Rick Santorum had previously said that he would, so it was entirely legitimate that a gay soldier, now protected by an act of Congress and signed by the President, would be curious about his fate in the military. To the credit of the candidates they all stood there like deer stuck in the headlights, but the mostly Tea Party crowd started booing the soldier for daring ask such a question and, in fact, for being himself. Not one of the Republican candidates for commander-in-chief displayed any leadership in face of this atrocious behavior - behavior that would have been deemed unpatriotic if the soldier were not gay. They simply stood there, frozen, not knowing what to do. These are the same people with the audacity to impugn the President's lack of leadership in the world. They could not even show the minimum leadership in face of a friendly domestic crowd. That incident will surely find its way in the 2012 campaign.

Well Mr. Baldasaro - remember him? This is a story about State Representative Baldasaro, from the great (and important to Presidential politics) state of New Hampshire, Mr. Baldasaro, not being content to simply ignore the booing like his favorite candidate, Rick Perry and all the others did, no, he added to the insult. He told ThinkProgress "He doesn't realize it, but when the shit hits the fan, you want your brothers covering your back, not looking at your back." Cute. The same could be said about women in the police force. Something like, "How can you fight crime with a woman partner when you're more concerned about her boobs than chasing crooks." I can only imagine what the press would do with a comment like that. But because it was said about a gay soldier, I guess it's quite alright since we know all gays are dying to get their grubby mitts on straight guys. Or so the preachers tell us.

But why is this even important? Another Neanderthal acting up? There are so many of them out there so why would anybody care? Well this particular Neanderthal happens to be the chairman of New Hampshire's Veteran Affairs Committee, the official government group paid with taxpayer dollars to serve as advocates for veterans. Predictably, Veterans organizations howled and are demanding his resignation from that position but this is not just a Veteran's matter. This is a serious matter that involves an entire political Party, the GOP which is incapable of standing up to the bigots in their group. They have tolerated the birthers who are thinly disguised racists, and now they are tolerating the homophobes. Haven't they heard they are on the wrong side of history? Don't they know that more and more young people don't really care about color or about sexual preference? Will they be eternally wedded to the 1950's?

What makes this even worse is that Baldasaro is Rick Perry's man in New Hampshire, a critical state for the Republican nomination, so he is actually influential with a potential Presidential candidate. Perry, of course will try to pretend nothing happened and hope it all blows away. And 50% of the time it does blow away because people have short memories and other more important things come up. But what could be more important than honoring the men and women who serve our country and are in harm's way? This may sound like a petty issue but it is not. It goes to the heart of who we are as a country. Will all sacrifice be honored equally or should we listen to Baldasaro's parting shot to the New Hampshire paper, the Eagle Tribune: "I thought the audience, when they booed, I thought it was great."

October 17, 2011

The Rumble in Vegas

The Republican Party is out of ideas. The debate last night in Las Vegas, while interesting in parts due to a few flare-ups between candidates was as stale as week old bread. The only way they are distinguishing themselves is through their relative personalities and personal attacks.

Rick Santorum, ever the moralist keeps reminding us he is morally superior to his colleagues. He's pro family as if there is anyone in America who is anti family. Even the gays are pro family but the likes of Santorum won't allow those types of people to have families. So much for pro family.

Ron Paul, bless him, is the only one who doesn't genuflect at the altar of the military industrial complex and wants to shut down all the bases we have in 150 countries around the world. Not a bad idea but the number probably should be a bit more modest. I'm thinking a dozen or so bases are probably needed for our military to be able to function. And then, there are the rather outlandish ideas like eliminating half of the federal departments, shutting down the Fed, and returning to the gold standard. Clearly nostalgia gone amok Sounds like good ideas but totally impractical in the modern world.

Newt Gingrich clearly the best debater in the bunch is having fun. He clearly knows he has no chance of winning so he is relaxed and makes his clever and sarcastic points. He is fun to watch because he has a sense of humor and clearly does what he wants, Answers the questions he wants to answer and is clearly having a good time.

Michele Bachmann is nothing but a string of clichés. Debate by bumper sticker. You can tell she memorized a bunch of canned slogans and spits them out whether they're relevant or not. She has got to be the worse statesperson on the podium. A kind of *anti-gravitas*. She exudes lack of confidence and looks desperate At least Sarah Palin usually sounds like she's in control even when spouting inanities. Bachmann is clearly over her head, even as a Representative in Congress. She should go back to being a tax adviser.

Herman Cain has what the Jews call *chutzpah*. He stands tall and weathers each storm with grace and humor. He is a natural leader. His only problem is that his ideas are well, Republican. He thinks poor people don't pay enough taxes and rich people deserve a bigger break. And he has the gall to accuse the Democrats of class warfare. He essentially told single mothers with children to raise who are scraping along with a waitress job that the country isn't balancing its books because they aren't contributing enough federal taxes. He even found a way to tax the homeless. Cain is all the proof you need that business men shouldn't become public servants. They are so wedded to the bottom line that they forget all those numbers on their spreadsheets represent real people's lives.

Rick Perry is another sort entirely. He is the classic used car salesman. It never ceases to amaze me how he deluded Texans to vote for him. I lived in Texas and I can assure you that Texans are not stupid. Some of them are yahoos, but even those aren't stupid. Perry strikes me as another version of a snake oil salesman turned revivalist, Elmer Gantry style for you older folks out there. There is clearly no substance there. He knows next to nothing about foreign policy and his domestic policy is to rape our country of every fossil fuel there is until we run out in 300 years. Where that sounds like a lot of time for most of us, it is a small amount of time with respect to civilization itself. Perry is an ode to selfishness and the wonton abandon of our land for whom many hold precious. He would gladly decimate our National parks and any part of America that might hold a drop of fossil fuel. Imagine a wildcatting cowboy in the White House. We survived eight years with a fake cowboy, now are we ready for the real thing?

Mitt Romney showed us he could dominate this motley crew. But what kind of feat is that? He easily dominated the hapless Perry who looked like he had been schooled, and he easily won the debate hands down. But what did he have to offer? Warmed over pabulum from the Bush years. Policies that we know failed miserably and gave us a huge recession. What Romney offers is more of the same, telling us that this time deregulation and tax cuts to millionaires is going to work. But we've seen this movie before and I'm not so sure that in spite of people's current frustrations they are wiling to go back to the Bush years.

That was the saddest assemblage of candidates ever. Maybe some of you remember the "nine dwarfs" when John Kerry ran for President? Folks had fun with that group because it was bereft of some of the heavies in the Democratic Party. But most of those "dwarfs" would wipe up the floor with this crew.

How low have the standards sunk.

October 19, 2011

Huntsman: The Forgotten Candidate

I watched Jon Huntsman on the Colbert Report last night and what I saw was a self confident intelligent man. I make a point to vote for intelligent people for President and basically ignore most of their positions. For example. my main objection to Michele Bachmann is not her issues although I don't agree with most of them. My objection to Bachmann is that she is as dumb as a doornail.

Most Presidents swallow their ideology when they take office anyway because they have to deal with reality, not issues in a vacuum. Reagan was against taxes but he raised them eight times. He also sold weapons to the Ayatollah because he thought that was the only way he could finance the Contras in Nicaragua. George W. Bush, a free marketeer initiated all the bailouts that Obama followed up on and ended up being blamed for, because Bush realized that was the only way to prevent the economy from total collapse.

Do you think the peacenik Ron Paul would hesitate for a second to retaliate against Iran if they had the gall to send a nuke our way? Presidents do what they have to do.

So my main criterion in the selection of a President is who is the smartest one in the bunch. Because a smart person will figure out a way to get out of the predicaments this messy world of ours brings our way.

I feel bad for Huntsman because he is stuck in a Party dominated by ignorance. While most of TV news tries, with varying degrees of success to educate the public, the folks at Fox do their level best to dumb down America. I have no problem with their right-wing bias. (I mean, let's face it, MSNBC has a left-wing bias) My problem is with their deliberate propagation of misinformation. It seems they are convinced that an ignorant America is more receptive to the conservative message. However, it is entirely possible to be a conservative and factually based. I used to listen to William F. Buckley with awe. Here was the conservative's conservative who rarely resorted to fabrication to make his points. I even found myself agreeing with him on occasion because his powers of persuasion were so strong.

I have the same feeling about Huntsman. He is a real patriot and basically an honest man, which is why Obama picked him to represent our country in China. The kiss of death, apparently for the Republican diehards who approach politics not as an exercise in patriotism but a kind of gruesome sporting event where winning is more important than helping one's fellow citizen. If Obama had to lose, I wouldn't mind so much if he lost to Huntsman.

But Huntsman has no chance in a Party that by and large does not believe in science, nor is open to facts. One thing is to be ignorant, it is quite another to be proud of it. And there is a significant number of Republicans that have fallen in that trap, and although I mentioned the obvious influence of Fox News, it is by no means the only culprit in the dumbing down of America. Talk radio has had a pernicious influence and the Supreme Court with its ruling that essentially classifies Corporations as People, has done untold damage to the Republic. [that is the genesis of the name of this blog]

Under these circumstances, an honest and intelligent man like Jon Huntsman has little chance in a Party dominated by no-nothings and do-nothings.

October 25, 2011

The Most Dangerous Man in America

If you ask conservatives who the most dangerous man in America is they will tell you billionaire George Soros, the man who goes around promoting democracy around the world. A little strange - I always thought conservatives supported that kind of thing. If you ask progressives the same question they will probably point to the billionaire Koch brothers, those spoiled brats who are determined to protect their billions from... I'm not sure exactly who. They have found a new toy to play with - Herman Cain - a willing servant of their *über* ambition.

But I would submit they are both wrong. The most dangerous man in America is hands down Frank Luntz. Dr. Lunz I should say. The mild mannered Luntz is an elitist's elitist. No Harvard or Yale for him. This patriotic American has a doctorate in politics from Oxford University in merry old England, the country we fought a revolution against.

Luntz has corporate clients all over the world but the two most relevant for this discussion are the Republican Party and its close affiliate, Fox News. And what makes him most dangerous is that unlike most Republicans and the Neo-Neanderthals at Fox, he actually believes in science, albeit in a kind of Dr. Frankenstein kind of way.

You see, we have all become used to the idea that polls are very suspect. A clever pollster can ask questions in a certain way as to elicit pretty much the response they want. It is a matter of how to phrase the question. You get very different answers if you ask if the government has a right to shoot an unarmed old man, than if you ask if our brave Navy Seals were justified in shooting Bin Laden.

But Lutz has taken polling to a whole new level. He has correctly found out using scientific methodology that people respond way more through their emotions than their intellect. (approximately 80% emotion and 20% intellect) so appealing to one's intellect (like I'm trying to do now) is a waste of time which is why I occasionally throw in a few emotional ditties.

So he has given up on trying to find out what people really want. What he does with the assistance of carefully chosen focus groups and sophisticated individual electronic dials is how people react to various situations and particularly to specific phrases. This is Goebbels on steroids. Goebbels, as propaganda Minister for the Nazis perfected what came to be called the "big lie". The idea being if you repeat a whopper enough times people start believing it. Luntz is not so crude. The beauty of his craft is that he actually scientifically tests the phrase which may be a lie or a half truth or even a truth that omits a bunch of mitigating other truths which might muddy the water. Simple clarity is the key. And these become the Republican talking points repeated *ad nauseum* on Fox.

What makes Luntz so dangerous is his scientific method. Republicans can go around deriding science - vaccinations, evolution, global warming, etc. but are thrilled to use scientific methodology when it suits their purpose.

Probably the most egregious example of Luntz's work is the phrase "government takeover of health care." This phrase was tested in Luntz's lab and received universal disdain. Luntz found a way to label Obama's health care reforms in a way the public would reject it out of hand without even knowing the particulars. It was so successful that people who support Medicare which is indeed government healthcare were against "Obamacare." There was that famous quip from the lady who yelled "Keep your government hands off my Medicare!" But it was only when my son-in-law repeated the phrase verbatim to me as if it was his own that I realized Luntz's evil genius. The amazing thing is that none of the conservatives seemed to notice that the progressive community was furious at Obama precisely because he didn't make the government take over the health care system which is what they really wanted. Obama merely reformed the private health care system, a fact that Luntz knows all too well and when asked he fudges the answer by saying he wants to "avoid" a government takeover. Sounds strangely similar to the justification for invading Iraq; that they **might** some day attack us with WMD.

Using this logic I would be entirely justified in blowing up my new neighbors because they have hunting rifles and some day they might come over and shoot me.

You can bet that Luntz will be in full form this election since it is increasingly hard for the Republican Party to sell Americans on the idea that billionaires deserve more and more protection from the rest of us, especially if they are asked to contribute a couple of percentage points more on their income taxes. But no worry, Luntz will be on the job and he will give Democrats a run for their money even if the public is about as low on Republicans as they were during the Depression. Science is a powerful thing, especially in the wrong hands.

October 27, 2011

The Price of Prejudice

Racism has been around since the founding of America, and although things have substantially improved, there are still reminders here and there. Much to the amazement of the rest of the world, America elected its first black President, but apparently there are people who have still not accepted that ground-breaking event. Accusing the President of not being American or being a closet Muslim is pure simple bigotry and in our age of political correctness the racists don't even have the backbone to admit their prejudice. They are only deluding themselves.

The dirty little secret is that racism is generally cost free. Preventing black people from eating at lunch counters doesn't cost much -- just people's dignity. Name-calling is pretty cheap, too. Segregated schools actually saves a few bucks. So by and large bigotry, even modern bigotry against homosexuals, the latest fad sanctioned by preacher prejudice, is essentially cost free.

The latest form of racism is not so much against blacks but against Latinos. All Latinos but especially Mexicans. And the reason is that there is a segment of that group that can be "legitimately" vilified. The **illegals**. And if you call them illegal aliens, they sound almost sinister, like the pod people.

Arizona, a state near the bottom in educational achievement, started the ball rolling. The state had to do something since the Federal Government decided it didn't want to turn America into a police state, so Arizona took a crack at it. Although the courts warned that a police state was not quite in line with the Constitution that didn't seem to deter other states from following Arizona's example.

Alabama, another state near the bottom of national scholastic achievement, decided to go Arizona one step better. Why stop at harassing the adults when you can harass their innocent children? Forcing schools to chase Latino kids sounded like a good idea to the new supermajority Republican state legislature. If you can't get to the parents going after their kids sounds brilliant to the racist mind. It is interesting to note that Texas Governor Rick Perry's numbers started to tank when he showed a scintilla of compassion towards the children of illegal workers. Texas, which has to actually live next to Mexico and is the beneficiary of illegal labor, is more reasonable towards the Latinos. First George W. Bush, and now Rick Perry. Maybe Texas being in the top tier of educational achievement helps. Who knows? Might be a coincidence.

In any case, Alabama, which apparently learned little from the George Wallace days, created conditions so onerous for the Latinos that they started to leave the state in droves. And guess what happened? There is nobody around to pick the fruit and vegetables so the Alabama farmers will be losing millions of dollars this year. Even next door Georgia will be losing millions as well. Of course, those of us who are not bigots could sit back and make fun of these ignoramuses -- say to ourselves they did it to themselves and revel in their misery. It is very tempting to look down at the redneck farmers going on TV complaining that they are about to lose their crops and think that if they only had a spine and stood up against the bigotry of their fellow citizens, they wouldn't find themselves in this predicament. But we can't sit back and revel because their collective hatred for Latinos is going to cost the rest of us as well. All that loss of food will drive up food prices for everybody else who has to pay the price to what amounts to colossal stupidity.

October 31, 2011

The Norquist Era Slowly Ending

When thinking about my previous article *"The Most Dangerous Man in America"* Grover Norquist was near the top of the list. He ended up runner-up to Frank Luntz. Where Luntz is the messaging genius, Norquist has had a strangle hold on the Republican Party for many years now.

As the founder of *Taxpayers for Tax Reform*, a misleading title if there ever was one, he exacts from Republican lawmakers a promise never to raise any type of revenue under any circumstances. One has to assume that includes an invasion from outer space. There is nothing reformist about forcing lawmakers to sign a pledge promising never to raise taxes which also includes closing tax loopholes for special interests.

America has had its share of bullies in the past, most notably Senator Joe McCarthy famous for destroying Hollywood careers and relentlessly persecuting innocent Americans. The good news is the era of bullies is coming to an end. Just ask the bullies who have ruled the Middle East with an iron fist. McCarthy himself was brought down when a few brave souls dared to call him out.

Bullies can only be brought to account when the people being bullied wise up and refuse to play along.

Norquist was always a mismatch for the new ultra Republican crowd. He's another elitist, much like Luntz. Norquist is from ultra-liberal Massachusetts, Harvard educated and married to a Muslim woman. This is the type of person the Tea Party types routinely deride without asking questions. Just imagine what the Republicans would do if Obama had married a Muslim woman, from Palestine, no less. Sarah Palin's hair would undoubtedly catch fire. For many Americans being married to a Muslim is not a big deal but for the fervently anti-tax pro-tea crowd that is akin to being a convicted felon.

But the good news for America is that Norquist's spell is starting to wear off.

Former Republican conservative Senator Alan Simpson got the ball rolling. On Lawrence O'Donnell's TV show, *The Last Word*, Simpson said:

" Why would anyone sign anything before they heard the debate, before they read the documents, before they did anything. But I'll tell you about Grover, if he's more powerful than the President of the United States, and when [Tom] Coburn nailed him [on ethanol subsidies], he said, if you're calling that a tax increase when you take away six billion in ethanol, that's ludicrous; it's also deceptive. And when we're digging in to those tax expenditures, and Grover and his happy band of warriors are trying to call that a tax increase, that's a damn lie, and he knows it. If he can get away with that, elect him president. But I'll tell

you one thing, the only thing that Grover can do to you...he can't kill you, he can't burn your house; the only thing he can do to you is defeat you for reelection. And if that means more to you than helping your country out of a terrible situation, you oughtn't to be there."

Just this week, forty brave House Republicans joined sixty Democrats sent a letter to the deficit super-committee telling them that "revenue increases" are fine with them. Just like the proverbial kid who intoned that the Emperor has no clothes, these heroic Republicans are sending an unmistakable message that the days of Norquist's blackmail are coming to an end. The enormity of the task is finally sinking in, and the country's welfare is finally starting to emerge as a higher priority than petty politics.

There of course is still plenty of time for the Congress to self-destruct, but the light is starting to look brighter at the end of the tunnel.

November 4, 2011

Right Wing in Retreat

After President Obama admitted to getting a "shellacking" in the 2010 election, it seemed that the Tea Party and their allies in the Republican Party were poised to dominate the national conversation. This emboldened the ultras on the Right to impose long held ideological positions. One of these newly minted governors, Scott Walker of Wisconsin was not happy with successfully negotiating with public unions. He decided to go for all the marbles by attempting to crush them as well. When his actions created a huge backlash, that should have been a warning to other governors to go slow with union reform.

But Governor John Kasich of Ohio wasn't paying attention or deliberately set out to test his state's voters. He went "all in" and proposed an anti-union law that was even harsher than Scott Walker's with the help of a complacent legislature. And it predictably backfired on him, in a big way. People in Ohio proved beyond a shadow of a doubt that the American electorate, although frustrated with the current economic conditions will not be fooled by extreme measures designed to hurt ordinary citizens. The tried and true tactic of scapegoating innocents during an economic crisis, a favorite of tyrants all over the world for as long as recorded history, just doesn't work well in America. American voters can be swayed with propaganda, with misleading statements, but it is hard to get Americans to punish their fellow citizens. That is a good lesson to learn for all politicians.

No matter what happens, Americans have a sense of fairness about them that is difficult to eradicate, which is why they don't see raising taxes a little bit on the richest 1% any sort of punishment as so many Republicans would like people to believe. Americans, by and large see this as an issue of basic fairness, just like repealing Kasich's union-busting law.

Another case of extremist rebuke yesterday was in Mississippi, that predictable conservative state. The proposal that "life begins at conception" sounds good as a sound bite and may make for a great bumper sticker, but as law is fraught with problems. That's what happens when people start believing in their own propaganda without regard to consequences.

Even though that law was resoundingly defeated in Colorado, the backers thought they had a shot in conservative and very pro-life Mississippi. Where the extremists went wrong is thinking that conservatives are necessarily thoughtless and mindless. That you could just push the right button and the "ditto-heads" as Rush Limbaugh calls them would just automatically vote like Pavlov's dogs. The problem is that people are not dogs and they think things through. The innocent sounding "life begins at conception" would not only ban abortions under any circumstances but also ban certain types of contraception, and jeopardize in vitro fertilization.

The moral of the story is twofold: 1) Most Americans, both Liberals and Conservatives dislike extremism of any kind and 2) American voters are lots more sophisticated than most politicians think they are. Sure there are still people who cling to irrational beliefs like Sarah Palin being qualified to being President of the United States, but fortunately for all Americans, as well as the whole world, these folks are in the minority and will stay that way for the foreseeable future.

November 9, 2011

Republican Darwinism

For a party that by and large repudiates Evolution, or Darwinism as they sometimes call it, Republicans seem to have no problem adopting Darwinism as an economic theory. Republican economics starts with the theories of British philosopher, Adam Smith, who published his seminal work, *The Wealth of Nations*, coincidentally in 1776. Although Smith predates Darwin, he eerily anticipates the concept of "survival of the fittest" as one of the core tenets of the Theory of Evolution.

When Mitt Romney says "markets work" he is absolutely right. Markets do indeed work. The Great Depression was a great example of the self correcting mechanism of markets. The only problem with "markets working" is that millions of people get devastated in the process. Romney's solution for the housing crisis is to let all the people struggling with their mortgages to just get kicked out of their homes. Again, markets do work, but not too well for the folks who land on the street. As for those of us in good shape, markets are terrific. Romney's solution for the insolvency of the auto industry was, again, the markets. Either the private sector could rescue the American auto giants or they would be allowed to just go belly up. A very neat solution. And since there were no private solutions to the auto crisis (or else they would have done so way before it got desperate) then

America would just have to stop making cars, as Ford, the only company that was still viable would have a tough time staying in business when the auto suppliers would be decimated as a result of GM and Chrysler going out of business.

The debate last night in Michigan, the home of the auto industry saved by President Obama, revealed that the solutions the Republicans have for our economy are: 1) Let everybody in trouble, including businesses big and small, go bankrupt, 2) lower taxes on corporations and rich people, 3) raise taxes on poor people, 4) do away with regulations that protect the public from any abuses emanating from the private sector, 5) fire as many public workers as possible, and 6) Get rid of Obama's Medical reforms.

And yes, it would work. Unemployment would rise to Depression levels, and thousands of businesses would close. All businesses surviving would trim down to basic levels and get stronger. America would become leaner and meaner. Unnecessary benefits such as Social Security and Medicare would be cut way back. Thousands of people denied medical treatment would simply die off, relieving society of those burdens.

This is essentially how evolution works. The weak die off, the strong get stronger and Nature (or God, if you prefer) takes care of all this with an invisible hand. Entire species get wiped out because they fail to adapt to new circumstances. It ain't pretty but it has been working for millions of years. Adam Smith coined the phrase "invisible hand" to explain how markets work and he was absolutely right. The only problem with that theory was that it worked so well that Great Britain's industrial revolution in the 19th century, which produced untold wealth also created a nightmare scenario for ordinary workers. But in Republicanland workers are simply cogs in the great Capitalist machine and should just be grateful for what they can get.

November 10, 2011

Sad State of Foreign Affairs

It was widely anticipated that Jon Huntsman would be the best of the Republican candidates for President on foreign policy in the last debate held in South Carolina. And he did not disappoint. He displayed his characteristic moderate approach as well as his vast knowledge particularly regarding relations with the Chinese. However, the surprise candidate was Rick Santorum, usually the dogmatic moralist, showing us a sophistication and courage that had not emerged before this debate. Most impressive was the mini-lesson he gave to his fellow Republican colleagues about the way foreign aid works. The caricature that has been circulating among Republicans for years is that foreign aid is some sort of welfare for hungry third world children. There is nothing that irritates Republican voters more than to think that their tax dollars are being wasted on the needy unwashed of the world. They can't stand welfare for their own people, much less any help for the other starving masses who inhabit the globe.

It is true that a tiny percentage of the foreign aid budget is used to send food to countries that are experiencing famine or population displacements due to catastrophes, both natural and man-made. Most of this aid is actually price support for American farmers and is part of the vast agricultural subsidies in which the government engages. But the great bulk of American foreign aid is in support of American arms manufacturers who are being subsidized since the foreign aid we send to allies like Israel, Egypt, and Pakistan is designated for their respective militaries to purchase armaments produced here at home.

Rick Santorum in a singular act of courage explained that simple reality to his fellow candidates, thereby undercutting the typical Republican narrative on the subject. Rick Perry, for the sake of a cheap applause line went so far as to say he would start foreign aid budgets at zero, including for that sacred cow, Israel. That line alone shows that Perry is not ready for the big dance. One cannot overstate what a colossal blunder that was.

The rest of the candidates took turns in proclaiming their "toughness" towards our enemies, trying hopelessly to portray Obama as a weakling. They took turns - with the exception of the perpetual peacenik Ron Paul - strutting their stuff about how they would handle Iran differently than Obama, all the while plagiarizing his policies for the audience, mostly unaware what they were proposing is exactly what Obama is doing. Santorum, praised Obama without naming him when he stated that someone is out there sabotaging Iran's nuclear ambitions, undercover no less. He went so far as to say that he "hoped" it was us. Gingrich sounded more like a right wing talk show bloviator than a Presidential candidate. But the worse one was Michele Bachmann who sits on the intelligence committee and therefore has access to Obama's major moves against Iran and said nothing except expectorating her usual slogans.

The sad part about this debate was that it shows how little importance is given to foreign policy by the American public. Even CBS chose to broadcast only the first hour of the debate, relegating the final half hour to the web. The Republican Party has returned to its lack of sophistication with regard to foreign policy. The last Republican President with real foreign policy credentials was George Bush the elder, George W. Bush apparently having learned next to nothing from his father.

If America is to be successful going forward in this increasingly interdependent world, we will need a leader who is savvy on the world stage. Based on their debate performance, this lot is by and large not ready for the job.

November 14, 2011

An Unlikely Hero

The soft-spoken and unassuming Senator from Rhode Island, Sheldon Whitehouse made a recent courageous and prophetic speech on the floor of the Senate. Nowadays with so much corrupting money in our political system, a politician can be called courageous just for telling a truth, even if it is somewhat self evident. Whitehouse simply and eloquently stated the case for climate change, or global warming if you prefer.

It is understandable that many religious people might be inclined to resist the evidence for Evolution because their religious beliefs tell them that humans are separate from Nature, separate from the animal kingdom itself since they collectively believe that people are endowed with a soul, which lower animals do not possess. Their religions therefore are wedded to the concept that we are special people put on this Earth for a higher purpose than simply reproducing and surviving. It is indeed a scary proposition to think that humans who have the capacity to create extraordinary art or excel at very complicated science are just simply animals who have evolved. It strikes at the core of many people's beliefs that they are separate and distinct from the animal kingdom, even though the evidence is compelling that we were part of a very long process of adaptation and survival.

But the deniers of climate change are not in the same category as ordinary folks who have a difficult time accepting that we share so many characteristics with giraffes and raccoons. The main reason researchers use mice in experiments, for example, in testing products for humans is that we share approximately 99% of our DNA with those creatures. This fact alone makes some people feel uneasy.

No such excuse is possible for deniers of human produced climate change. Perhaps it is easier to convince Evolution deniers that human produced climate change does not exist since there is considerable overlap between these two groups. However, climate change denying is an industry, a well orchestrated and well-funded industry financed by, well, industry itself. Millions of dollars have been invested by polluting companies to convince us that climate change is either not occurring or humans have nothing to do with it.

How this became an obsession among conservatives is rather obvious. Conservatives tend to blindly support big business. I recall with disgust when Representative Joe Barton, Republican from Texas, publicly apologized to BP for the negotiation by President Obama for a 20 billion dollar fund to mitigate the results of their oil spill in the Gulf of Mexico. With leaders of this low caliber it not surprising that there is an organized effort to exempt the planet polluters from taking responsibility for their actions. The Republican Party as a whole has not only fought tooth and nail to protect these folks from paying their fair share of taxes but also to prevent any consequences for their share of climate change.

Sheldon Whitehouse will go down in history as one of the few brave souls who bucked the moneyed interests in favor of his country and the planet itself. Will that be sufficient to stem the tide? Or will he be relegated to obscurity as another voice in the wilderness crying out against corruption, greed, and irresponsibility? Only time will tell.

November 17, 2011

A Modest Proposal

The following proposal is inspired by the wisdom of Newt Gingrich with apologies to Jonathan Swift.

Mr. Gingrich has proposed relaxing the ban on hiring children in order to give them opportunities to clean their school, replacing union protected maintenance workers. Mr. Gingrich is on the right path but out of a sense of great modesty and his great sensitivity to our politically correct culture he does not go far enough.

First of all, the amount of work available to children at school is limited. Miss Schultz's second grade class could probably take care of the whole school thus depriving the other children the chance of becoming productive members of society. To be fair, Mr. Gingrich did suggest flipping hamburgers as a suitable task for kids, but only 12 year olds and older would be suitable for such a demanding job. How about the millions of 7 to 11 year olds? Even 5 and 6 year olds? Where would they go to initiate their "process of rising"?

Surely if the President can appoint a commission to work on our debt problems, a parallel commission could be appointed to solve the child unemployment problem. Most people are unaware that among certain groups of children, the unemployment rate is almost 100%!

Employing children would solve so many problems. First of all, it would solve the problem of children's entitlement attitudes. Some kids are convinced that their parents are solely responsible for their economic well-being. This creates a culture of dependency that sometimes takes them into adulthood. What adult has not been sickened by kids begging their parents for totally unnecessary things like toys and the like. It is high time that children pull their own weight and stop with the cry-baby attitude.

Secondly, there are jobs just too dangerous for adults. Why waste a perfectly good adult when you can get a kid to do it? There are so many opportunities in testing products, high risk jobs like walking the high beams on skyscrapers or even dismantling high explosives. Their delicate little hands are surely more adept at working with tricky mechanisms, microchips, and so much more detail work. During World War II American industry found that women were actually better than men at certain industrial jobs where manual dexterity was key. But how about kids? Children have their reflexes intact, have better hand and eye coordination and would be better than even women at repetitive menial tasks.

But the most important problem child labor would solve is our current lack of competitiveness vis-á-vis China and India. For example, the biggest competitive advantage the Chinese have over the United States is a labor force that works for next to nothing without any rights whatsoever -- the corporate dream environment.

Karl Marx must be smiling in his grave thinking that the Communist Party in China produced a more ruthless work environment for workers than 19th century England, about which he wrote his famous Communist Manifesto. The Chinese have outdone the English and then some. All of our problems would be solved if we would replace the existing workforce with children. No minimum wage. In some cases we could experiment with no wages at all since we know the proclivities of some children to wallow in candy and video games. There is little chance the Chinese worker could underbid our children. They would be unable to compete against a workforce able to work for gum.

Therefore, as an adjunct to the debt commission President Obama, following the wise counsel of Mr. Gingrich, should announce a Commission chaired by Dick "Darth Vader" Cheney, and Grover "no taxes" Norquist (why bother with Democrats - they will only gum up the works) and get to work on a plan that would gradually replace most of the American workforce with children. Children could be organized into classes, pretty much along the existing class system so beautifully enforced by the schools. Entry level jobs would start with Kindergarten where the work would not be too demanding and the kids would therefore work for free. As children progress up the class level the rewards could get more substantial. First graders would be able to work for candy, second graders would work for Happy

Meal prizes and so forth. Each job would be age appropriate as well as its corresponding remuneration.

Soon, the United States would have the cheapest labor force in the world and be able to beat the Chinese (and others) at their own game. It would be truly a new golden era.

November 21, 2011

Dirty Little Secret

Can we finally say that the Republican Party is not interested in retaking the White House? This is not some nefarious strategy concocted by the likes of Karl Rove, Dick Army, and other conspiratorial big wigs. I'm sure they among other Republican leaders would enjoy having a fellow traveler in the White House if for no other reason than to be invited to fancy parties and to participate in developing policies.

No, in this case, the fish is not rotting from the top, it is rotting from the bottom. Yes, I am talking about the Republican rank and file, the ones who make the final determination in a democracy. How else to explain the rotation of the greatest nincompoops in the history of the GOP to the top of the popularity polls, and the total snubbing of the few decent candidates who are actually in the race?

Let's start with the case of Michele Bachmann who is one therapy session away from being placed in a psychiatric institution. Maybe "insane" is too strong a word, but the more politically correct "challenged" is not. Bachmann is challenged on so many levels, factual, theoretical, political, philosophical and even religious. She is a walking bag of contradictions who is not even qualified to be in Congress, much less to be leader of the free world. She has less basic knowledge than Sarah Palin, who in a surprising intelligent move decided not to embarrass herself by running.

Bachman is a hopeless paranoid who makes Joe McCarthy look like a reasonable man. Her ideas of governance are so out there, that if she were a baseball player they would have to place her in the parking lot because her views do not even fit in the ball park. Why anybody would take her seriously will always remain a mystery to me, but there she was, riding on top of the heap as if she was a serious contender for the job.

Then there was the curious case of Donald Trump, that over-inflated egomaniac who also topped the list at some point.

His sweepstakes ticket was to concoct a phony investigation into the President's birth, complete with non-existent investigators conducting a counterfeit investigation which produced no results. This is world class leadership? Still, it did not prevent him from rising to the top albeit temporarily. Thanks to an assist by the rational media, he was appropriately laughed off the stage.

And then there was the dude from Texas who makes George W. look brilliant. Where were the Dixie Chicks when we needed them? I guess their appetite for politics diminished when they got savaged for expressing shame over their lame ex-governor. The current governor, Rick Perry, who was the temporary hope of the Republican primary voting claque, turned out to be the fruitcake that many Texans secretly knew he was but were too mortified to admit in public. I'm sure in private they were slapping their thighs with perhaps the perverse pleasure of pulling a fast one on the rest of us. As George W. wisely said, "fool me once, shame on – shame on you. Fool me – you can't get fooled again."

And how about the pizza man? Forget about his dalliances with women which would be forgiven if he had something to offer the nation besides that ridiculous slogan that sounds like that Nazi in the movie "Inglorious Basterds". (You'll have to look that one up.) Herman Cain was a joke from the start, a kind of lesser Ross Perot without the funny ears and vast knowledge of economics charts. Who in their right mind would think that a guy who ran a pizza chain would have the chops to meet with world leaders and not be made the butt of everyone's joke? Apparently many Republican voters did because he made it to the top of the list too.

So now we're down to the last two contenders, both representing the corruption and bankruptcy of our current political class. If cream floats to the top, these two are indeed way past their consumable date. Newt Gingrich not only resigned in disgrace from being Speaker of the House, but shamelessly profited largely by abusing his former position to make millions. Sure, strictly speaking, he was not a lobbyist. Being a lobbyist is seemingly too honorable a profession for the likes of Newt. You have to be registered, and go through all kinds of pesky disclosures, and your activities need to be transparent. There are many lobbyists who serve a very vital function. Generally they are knowledgeable in specialized areas and can help refine and explain complex legislation to Congressional staffers. But this occupation is too mundane for the erudite Dr. Newt. He would never sully himself with the crassness of dealing with technical matters. No, Dr. Newt is a big picture (read big money) man. His quasi-lobbying was more along the lines of giving advice such as who is vulnerable to what type of threat and how to buy off a congressman. Did I say "buy off"? I meant "influence." That's why Gingrich gets the big bucks, because he flies above the radar screen (or is it below?) and gives the client the needed knowledge to ward off all those inconveniences associated with following the law. What a terrific choice for President! Don Corleone as commander-in-chief.

And now for the *pièce de résitance*, Mitt Romney, the perennial, the eternal seeker of higher office. Romney has a slightly different form of corruption than Gingrich. Whereas Gingrich is a shameless moneygrubber, Romney is the blue-blood of the bunch. If we allowed nobility in this country, Romney would be Sir Willard, Count of Cambridge. But he had to content himself with the obligatory silver spoon with his oatmeal, I mean porridge. He fits right in with the beer-swilling Tea Party types. Maybe if he gets to the White House he might invite his new Tea Party buddies to his country club to sip a few Manhattans. His corruption of the body politic is, of course, his ability to adapt to any circumstance. He is the ever changing, ever slippery politician. Ted Kennedy famously said it best, "I'm pro-choice and Mitt is multiple choice." The ever unctuous Romney gives empty suits a bad name. He is the embodiment of what the Tea

Party claims they hate. He has no core, no principles, except for the sacrosanct profit motive. His claim to fame was that he turned a profit on the Olympics, just what the Ancient Greeks had in mind for the noblest of amateur endeavors. But as Governor of Massachusetts, he ranked 47th out of 50 in job creation, not so great a track record for a guy claiming to be a "job creator". Of course job creation is the furthest thing from the mind of a man who made a fortune cannibalizing companies and putting workers out on the street. If this is the guy who will turn our economy around, we are in deeper trouble than we thought.

Now the Republican base could be forgiven if these were the only people in the running for their Party's nomination. (I deliberately left out Ron Paul, because…well, everybody else does) And little can be said about Rick Santorum since he suffers from periodic spasms of good sense combined with bouts of sanctimony without having caught on with either the sensible or the sanctimonious. But no, there are more. It seems like the only candidates with a legitimate shot at the Presidency and who might do a reasonable job of it have been marginalized by the Republican electorate.

The first is Tim Pawlenty who had a decent run as Governor of Minnesota, and is able to speak in coherent paragraphs. Pawlenty had the distinction of running a generally Democratic State as a Republican without being the subject of a recall election. He is a conservative without being a fanatic. But the voters did not give him much of a chance. He stood out among the weirdoes and creeps. Lately, however, he lost a bit of his shine by signing up with the Romney machine hoping to be Vice-President. He should have held back and tried again next time but it seems the lure of power was too much for him. Too bad because he was one of the good ones.

The second candidate is Jon Huntsman, already the topic of a previous article (Huntsman: the Forgotten Candidate).

Another reasonable Republican who not only made the unfortunate mistake of telling the public he believed in science, but also having made the worse mistake of serving his country under the dastardly Barack Obama. Republicans might have forgiven his flirtation with science, but his working for the ignominious Obama who, according to some Republicans, is the worst President in the history of the Republic (worse than Millard Fillmore?) was just too much to bear.

The third candidate is Buddy Roemer who most people don't even know is running. Roemer has the dubious distinction of not only scoring low with his fellow Republicans but not even being invited to any of the debates. Sure, we are all fascinated with the ramblings of the crazy lady and the pizza man, but a guy who served in Congress and was the successful governor of Louisiana, well that's just one too many people to keep track of. And here is the kicker.

Roemer, who is not generally a one issue type, is emphasizing the issue of our time, the explosion and corrupting influence of big money in our politics. One would think the Tea Party folks would be interested in that huge issue, and embrace a candidate who has proven he can work with Republicans and Democrats and is all about reducing corruption of the political system. I suppose they never received that memo from their patron saint, Dick Armey, the king of big money, so poor Buddy gets relegated to the bottom of the heap.

So what to make of all this? The unmistakable conclusion is that the Republican voters really don't want to take back the White House. All that talk of taking back their country is just talk. They seem to be happy with Obama in charge. He makes such a convenient target. Conservatives have been warning us for a while now that the great economic meltdown is coming. Patriotic Americans should be stockpiling gold and guns, because we are on the verge of collapse under the weight of Obama's shoving Socialism down our throats. Maybe the true believers live the fantasy that when the apocalypse comes in 2012, prepared Republicans will be able to take over this county by force and impose a type of Reich (Reich is aptly a cognate of the English word Rich) in America with a true Tea Party Patriot at the helm. (Sound familiar?) What if the economy doesn't disintegrate? The joke's on them.

December 3, 2011

Newt's Woman Problem

This blog tries to avoid the salacious side of politics. It was just too cheap to dwell on Herman Cain's marital infidelity so it was basically ignored here. Generally speaking, personal matters should stay personal. The spectacle of the Republican Party dragging President Clinton through the mud over the Lewinsky affair was a colossal waste of time, energy and money and ultimately produced nothing but a lot of smoke.

However, Newt Gingrich's problem is different. Whereas Herman Cain is clearly a womanizer, he fits the traditional model of married men fooling around, but remaining basically (in their own way) loyal to their spouse. Tawdry yes, but rather pedestrian as a public issue. Of course, it goes without saying that to the wives who endure these are not "issues" but small and large betrayals they have to deal with in the best way they can.

Gingrich's womanizing is (much like everything else about him) in a separate category. He actively sought out mistresses that were in some way "better" than his current wife. That is not really "fooling around" but full-fledged treachery. For many women, these are not important distinctions. To most women, taking your secretary to bed after a wild office party is just as repugnant as a full blown long term affair, but as a matter of public scrutiny of a potential President there is a very significant difference.

Many Presidents have had various dalliances with the ladies, most notoriously Bill Clinton, LBJ, Jack Kennedy, and the most straight-arrow, Ike. Even the angelic Jimmy Carter admitted to Playboy magazine he committed adultery in his heart. We don't elect saints to the highest office -- we elect leaders -- men (so far) with colossal egos and, consequently, colossal appetites.

But Newt is in a class of his own. The sex is almost a minor footnote. This is beyond "flip-flopping," of which he is also guilty. (More to come on that subject) This is perfidy of the highest order. This a man who cannot be trusted. This is flip-pancy taken to the extreme and it is reflected in his politics. His comment in Saturday night's debate about the Palestinians being "an invented people" is the kind of light-minded slur that has serious international consequences. Maybe the yahoos in the Republican Party enjoy that kind of smear, but this is not the kind of statement that should be coming from the leader of the free world, not to mention the leader of the country that has been trying to broker a peace between Palestinians and Jews for decades. His glib comment about President Obama was vintage Newt: "What if [Obama] is so outside our comprehension, that only if you understand Kenyan, anti colonial behavior, can you begin to piece together [his actions]? That is the most accurate, predictive model for his behavior." Not only is this comment inaccurate, it is frivolous and gratuitous, totally beneath an aspiring world leader. Of course the fact that it is plagiarized from Dinesh D'Souza, a former Ronald Reagan speech writer and full-time dingbat, is only frosting on the cake.

Also there is the problem with Newt's current wife. Americans in general are quite forgiving but also have strong feelings about their first lady. One might argue about the relative importance of a President's wife, but there is a long-standing tradition in this country about the prominent role of the first lady. Calista, his current wife, does not fit the moral standards of many Americans. And this is not a conservative or liberal issue. Many Americans will not be enchanted with a first lady who was a mistress, a "home wrecker." This may or may not be fair but it is one of those realities that will hit home sooner or later.

Gingrich's behavior towards women is important. It illustrates his public behavior. It shows us an egocentric, arrogant individual who is superficial and devoid of morality. Not exactly what we need in a President at this juncture in our history. He is the embodiment of that old WWII slogan about loose lips sinking ships. This is not a man who should be trusted with our country's most sensitive secrets.

December 13, 2011

Newtonian Justice

Newt's at it again. This time it's the judges. Quite a bad lot he claims; just can't trust them to go your way. Independent minded types. One day they're handing the Presidency on a silver platter to a guy who didn't win it fair and square and on another occasion they force dark skinned children to go to school with light skinned kids. What a zany bunch, as Mitt would say. You never know how they will shake out.

Following the Constitution is a mucilaginous undertaking. The framers didn't make it easy on successive generations. All that vague language, and those principles! Tricky stuff. So to make it to the Supreme Court you have to be extra smart. I mean really smart. Better than game show smart. Then when you come down with a decision the country will wow in amazement. But believe it or not, though, not everybody is dazzled by your brilliance. Occasionally, as with the *Brown vs. the Board of Education* decision, where the Court abolished the obviously oxymoronic "separate but equal" laws in some of the southern states that separated kids by race in schools, some folks were not entirely pleased. And when that decision enabled the Civil Rights movement, some people were downright outraged. That's when the term "activist judges" came into existence.

Those damn judges and their activism. And it was a 9-0 decision. None of those namby-pamby 5-4 decisions where modern day justices vote for their team. In the "old" days of 1954, judges, exhibited real independence, actually followed the Constitution, and had real spines.

But then came the dreaded *Roe vs, Wade* decision which was the last straw for the conservative team. Pro-choice was born. Women were permitted to make up their own minds about whether to have or not to have an abortion. That is when the term "activist judges" became the rallying cry for the right in America. A dog whistle that every conservative politician knows how and when to blow.

So Newt, the all zany, all the time candidate chooses to blow it as hard as he can the eve of the Iowa caucuses. But he doesn't leave it to chance. Any run-of-the-mill Republican knows how to invoke the activist judges clarion call. Newt, always in a class of his own, has to take it to the limit. As President he would cut the courts down to size. Predictably liberal courts would be abolished and the judges would be presumably sent to Guantanamo with all the other terrorists. Only conservative courts would remain and the Supreme Court justices would have to watch their step or President Newt (has a nice ring to it, *n'est pas?*) would haul them into hearings and force them to explain themselves. Joe Stalin would be proud.

According to Newtonian philosophy, the courts have just too damn much power. Kind of reminds me of the "rent too damn high" guy. So in order to rectify the country we have to (slightly) violate the Constitution (makes sense if you don't think too hard). When it is convenient conservatives have no problem violating the Constitution or running roughshod on people's liberties or states rights or whatever works for them. Because when they do it, it's for the benefit of the country, When the liberals do it is always self-serving.

Take the Terry Schiavo case. The party of personal responsibility, family values and states rights pushed a case to the Supreme Court in order to force her family to do what a group of strangers wanted for her rather than follow her and her husband's wishes. That is judicial activism to the extreme.

Of course the most egregious and most activist decision of all time was the recent *Citizen United* decision where the Supreme Court deemed corporations to be people (spot a trend?). This decision has resulted in an avalanche of unrestricted, unreported, and secret big money that only benefits the hugely affluent. When President Obama correctly predicted an opening of the floodgates of big money in our elections, Justice Alito in a facial gesture of pure contempt for the President, did his version of the now infamous "you lie" outburst by Representative Joe Wilson. Not only is Justice Alito an activist Justice in his voting record but he has crossed into pure politics by visibly reacting in public to the President's State of the Union address, an act without precedent. This is judicial activism taken to a new level.

But Newt is not talking about Alito. Or Scalia. Newt likes their kind of activism. If Justice Scalia announced that Obama was a terrible President or one who consistently violates the

Constitution, Newt would be thrilled and probably announce that the Court has finally come to its senses. Newt doesn't really object to activism on the part of the courts. His problem is with **liberal** activism, or any activism with which he doesn't agree. That's nice work if you can get it, but it is not what the Supreme Court, or any court for that matter, is designed to do. The Constitution provides for checks and balances between the three branches of government, a system that has served us well for over two hundred years, but Newt, that old-fashioned bully is not content with just impersonating Don Corleone, a fictional character, but rather, focusing on his credentials as a historian, he seems to be channeling the very real Joseph Stalin.

December 20, 2011

Rheumatic Republicans

The Affordable Care Act, derided as Obamacare by conservatives has become a rallying cry for all Republican candidates for President. They all line up, sheep-like, to promise a gullible public that the repeal of the most profound act favoring the middle class since FDR enacted Social Security will solve most of their problems.

How did this happen? How did this Act which was designed to help ordinary folks become so controversial? It is easy to blame the usual suspects, Fox News, Rush Limbaugh, Glenn Beck, and others making money off people's anxieties, but there is much more to it than that. This blog has previously exposed evil genius Frank Luntz who coined the focus group tested phrase "government takeover" (see "The Most Dangerous Man in America"). And Sarah Palin's clever "death panels" quip certainly didn't help much to warm up Americans to health care reform.

The sad truth is that there are a large number of Americans who are suspicious of government - any government - practically to the point of paranoia, that they are willing to believe anything people say as long as it's negative. What other explanation is there? We live in an age of information. It took me less than three minutes to find out the particulars of the Affordable Care Act. You don't have to read hundreds of pages of legalese to get the main points of it. Compounding the problem, the Act is being phased in over four years to accommodate the needs of private insurance companies to gear up. And, yes, health care in America with the exception of the VA and Medicare is in the hands of the private insurance companies, much to the chagrin of the true left wingers who really wanted a government takeover. That they didn't get it seems to be lost in the political noise machine.

I'm wondering out loud how many Americans actually know what's in the Act. They may have heard about private insurance companies being prohibited from refusing people with pre-existing conditions in the near future, a huge concession on the part of the insurance companies which had to be balanced by the imposition of an individual mandate. It's almost comical that the Republicans, the party of personal responsibility, would be against a provision that requires people to be responsible for their own health care. Without an individual mandate it is the rest of us who become responsible for saving uninsured people's lives.

But let's forget the future for a bit. Let's review what the Affordable Care Act is doing this year, 2011, as we speak.[1]

First, 2.5 million more young adult Americans automatically qualify for insurance. Thanks to a provision in the law young adults can be part of their parents insurance up to age 26. Not a

---

[1]   Affordable Act Details Source: Kathleen Sibelius

big deal if you are not in those circumstances but certainly a big deal if you are and your kid needs health insurance.

Second, prior to the Affordable Care Act insurance companies in too many states were able to raise their rates without explaining their actions. Now, insurers who want to hike their rates by 10% or more have to explain and justify those increases in writing. Experts will scrutinize those explanations and, in many cases, can tell the insurer to reduce their price. As a result of this law, over the last year, 42 states, the District of Columbia and the five U.S. territories have stiffened their oversight of proposed health insurance rate increases. Results are beginning to come in. For example, Connecticut's Insurance Department rejected a 20% rate hike by one insurer; Oregon chopped the rate increase by one of its largest insurers almost in half, saving money for 60,000 citizens.

Third, a new consumer protection took effect in 2011 called the 80/20 rule. This makes sure that at least 80% of your premium dollars are being spent on health care and improving your care – not on advertising and executive salaries. If your insurer fails this test, you get a rebate, starting this summer, This rule makes sure that you get your money's worth from your health insurance company.

Fourth, under the Affordable Care Act, most families are eligible for free preventive services. You may now have access to free preventive services such as:

Blood pressure readings, cholesterol tests, and nutrition counseling Many cancer screenings, including mammograms and colonoscopies. Flu and pneumonia shots. Routine vaccinations against diseases such as measles, hepatitis, and meningitis.

Fifth, Medicare beneficiaries now also have access to free preventive measures like physicals, flu shots, tobacco cessation programs, mammograms, and colonoscopies. Medicare will cover an annual wellness visit with no charge to seniors. And thanks to the new health law, the Medicare prescription drug coverage gap known as the donut hole is starting to close. Through the end of October, 2.65 million people facing the donut hole in Medicare have received discounts on brand name drugs. These discounts have saved seniors and people with disabilities a total of $1.5 billion on prescriptions – averaging about $569 per person.

Sixth, the number of doctors, nurses, and health care professionals in the National Health Service Corps has nearly tripled in the last three years. For the first time in its forty year history the National Health Service Corps can count more than 10,000 members in its ranks.

Seventh, in April 2011 the Partnership for Patients launched. This is a national partnership that will help save 60,000 lives in the next three years by preventing medical errors. The Partnership for Patients also has the potential to save up to $50 billion in Medicare over the next 10 years. More than 6,500 partners – including over 2,900 hospitals as well as physicians and nurses groups, consumer groups, and employers – have pledged their commitment to the Partnership for Patients.

Eighth, the Affordable Care Act has brought strong tools to fight fraud. In 2011, the Department of Justice recovered more than $5.6 billion in fraud government-wide. Of the $5.6 billion, $2.9 billion was in health care fraud alone. Providers now have to go through tougher screening procedures before they can start billing Medicare. Investigators have been given new tools that allow them to analyze data in order to identify and stop suspicious payments before they go out. As part of the law, new rules were released that will give states the flexibility to recover improper Medicaid payments, saving more than $2 billion over the next five years, with nearly $1 billion going back to the states.

How many people would be against all that is happening right now, with more to come next year and three years after that? How is this unconstitutional – as the favorite new conservative epithet goes? As stated earlier, I wonder how many people even know these basic facts?

So the spectacle of Newt Gingrich and Mitt Romney, previous supporters of health care reform falling all over themselves to deny what they had previously endorsed would be almost comical if it were not so sad. But Newt and Mitt are not leaders, they are slavish followers of the mob mentality orchestrated by a few slick operators intent on destroying this President. I don't really blame operatives like Dick Army and his Astro Turf minions so much. We all live in a democracy, after all, and even the most obnoxious have a right to their opinions. Rather, it is the people who are responsible for the politicians' clownish behavior, For example, a recent study conducted by Fairleigh Dickinson University demonstrated that followers of Fox News were more ignorant of current events than people who didn't watch any news at all. Let's all hope and pray for good old fashioned American common sense to take hold. The country sorely needs it.

December 28, 2011

Who Cares About Iowa?

Loyal readers of this blog might remember a post written on October 12 entitled "Tea Party Sells Out" where the proposition was made that after all the gnashing of teeth about not settling for mere electability, the Tea Party would ultimately support the ultimate empty suit, Mitt Romney.

Republicans are so predictable. They always support retreads, losers. Whoever is next in line, like robots. Bold moves, change?

Poppycock.

Republicans just want things as they were. Lets go back to the *status quo* under George W. Things were so much better. The country was debt free, we were at peace, and the jobs kept rolling in. Just what we need, another 'W'. And if things don't work out, we can always get another Democrat in there to bail us out and complain about how he's bailing us out and being so reckless and wimpy. Sounds like a plan.

So what happened in Iowa? Well, the princess of Iowa got her clock cleaned. She went from Tea Party darling, winning the Iowa straw poll (now I know why they call it "straw") to Ms. 5%. Five percent? Joe the Plumber could get 5%! Not to insult Iowa Republicans or anything, but aren't they just a bunch of dingbats? Even bigger dingbats than the queen of dingbats, Michele herself. How does one go from peach to leech in a few short months? Did she change substantially? Did they find out she cheated on her taxes, her husband? I mean she was always quirky. She always had that annoying voice and little depth. I thought that's what they liked about her. Clean slate. Redo Washington from scratch, in the image of the Tea Party. The good Iowa folk just couldn't pull the trigger on Ms. Bachmann. Just too weird for their taste. And of course, the dirty little secret is that they don't care too much for women leaders. You know it says so in the Bible. Women must obey their husbands and they were afraid when they got a hard look at that creepy husband of hers. We're going to elect her and he's going to be there flitting about, telling her what to do. I'm only guessing.

We know what happened to Perry and Gingrich, though. They were just the flavors of the week. Perry already seems to be resigned to the fact that he really belongs back in Texas. (I'm not so sure he's getting such a hearty welcome back.). Perry seems to have exhibited some intelligence and sees his path fairly clearly. But not Newt. No sirree. Newt is convinced that he got robbed. If only he didn't have all this hefty baggage to contend with he would be flying first class. Sign of the times, Newt. You have to pay extra for baggage these days – that's how they roll. But no matter. The self-appointed Pudgy Rocky isn't a quitter. He just lost the first round but he didn't throw any punches. Apparently he learned from Mohammed Ali the old "rope a dope" strategy. Let them wallop you into a corner and when they tire of all this pummeling you get them when they're not looking. Hey, it worked for Ali, why not the pudgy kid? Can't wait to see the Newt come out swinging against Mitt. I mean, doesn't it sound like a comedy team? Newt and Mitt. Kind of like Mutt and Jeff, for you old timers out there. Kids, look it up.

What can you say about Ron Paul? He has his fans. The unlikely rock star. He appeals to the youth of America – he's going to legalize drugs and end wars and save America. Wow, what a guy. That's enough to make us forget he wants to abolish the Federal Reserve and return to the gold standard. (In a sentence, the gold standard is impractical in that it ties our economy to a fixed amount of gold, thereby inhibiting its growth.) Paul's real agenda is to cut the Federal Government way back to 19th century levels, a pipe dream if there ever was one. Of course, there's plenty more to concern ourselves with Paul – his intemperance, his flirtation with racism. He even has second thoughts about the Civil Rights act. After all, as a true Libertarian he doesn't believe government has much to say about anything. So if folks want to relegate black people to the back of the bus, or create segregated dining rooms, so be it. And if a black man gets half a white man's wage, just for being black, well, *c'est la vie*. But the young folks rarely get to hear this less pleasant message. That's more for the old folks back home. Still, Paul has a consistent twenty-ish percent following come hell or high water, and they are just devoted to him.

And how about the hapless Huntsman? He just doesn't fit in with this "new" Republican Party. OK, he didn't really campaign in Iowa, but he wouldn't have gotten much more than the one percent he received. Amazing, since he is the only Patriot in the bunch choosing to serve his country in spite of the President being from that "other" Party. That will teach him to be patriotic. Next time he should just thumb his nose if a Democratic President invites him to serve his country.

And I don't even want to talk about Buddy Roemer. How pathetic he got less votes than the absent pizza man. And of course, the press will crown Rick Santorum the true winner. (they hate Romney that much). But how predictable was that? Santorum just grabbed the Pat Robertson/Mike Huckabee slot. The religious fanatics need their own personal candidate, and God bless them, they don't care if he is qualified or has a shot. He has to say all the right buzzwords and have no obvious baggage. Santorum can be relied upon to speak like a preacher although he just plays one on TV. These are the same people who would have happily put Pat Robertson in the White House.

The guy who said that God was punishing New York City for its sins as an explanation for 9/11. When the Reverend Wright said essentially the same thing the press crucified him and tried to blame Obama for what he said. But Pat gets a pass, because, well, he's good old Pat who says the darnedest things like blaming New Orleans for Hurricane Katrina. Yeah, God does indeed work in mysterious ways. Still can't figure out what New Orleans did to deserve that. So Santorum has the evangelical (white, let's not forget that) vote sewn up. Sometimes we forget there's a black evangelical vote that doesn't go for these off-beat characters like Pat Robertson. Santorum is ill prepared for a Presidential campaign, not even for a primary. If someone lays a few million on him right now he won't know what to do with it. He's running a Mom and Pop shop and wants to play CEO with the big boys. But never mind, the good Christian folks of Iowa don't mind if he flames out, they got their licks in and once more proved their irrelevance to the process of electing the leader of the free world.

In sum, Iowa was a predictable exercise in futility, and a pseudo nail-biter for political junkies. Once again, it served to confirm the obvious that Republicans are risk-adverse boring people who haven't a clue about leadership but have the gall to complain about the lack of leadership in Congress. Look in the mirror, Iowan Republicans, you have found the problem and the problem is you.

January 4, 2012

Ron Paul's Excellent Adventure

It's time to take Ron Paul seriously. With his strong second finish in New Hampshire following his virtual three-way tie with Romney and Santorum in Iowa he has earned the title of strongest alternative to Mitt Romney. But surprisingly, the one thing that both liberal commentator Ed Schultz and conservative commentator Rush Limbaugh agree on is that Paul doesn't count. In fact all the media, left, right and center have generally ignored Paul. The results from New Hampshire were pretty predictable except for Rick Perry, who just loved the state so much that he was schoolgirl giddy when he discussed its motto, "Live Free or Die." I wonder what Perry thinks of New Hampshire now with his 1% showing.

When candidate Paul does this well, however, it seems important to try to understand what he stands for and also what his fans think he stands for. Make no mistake, most politicians have supporters, Paul has fans. And, in keeping with how most fans behave. Paul's fans have a blind spot for anything that could be construed as negative about their hero.

The key word that defines Ron Paul is "liberty". This is the banner under which he stands. But liberty - something all Americans love - has different meanings. Liberty isn't always a good thing. Many young people hear liberty and think freedom to smoke pot or engage in marginal behavior. They may not have given much thought to the debate exchange about a young man with no medical insurance being left to die due to his poor choices. After some in the crowd yelled "yeah!" indicating they agreed with the premise, Paul felt embarrassed and mumbled that when he was working for a Catholic hospital, they did charity work and didn't turn down anyone. This is worthy of a Charles Dickens novel.

Ron Paul essentially wants to roll back the clock to the 19th century. Minimal taxes and minimal government. He is counting on people's general lack of knowledge of history. In the 19th century charities did the best they could to alleviate human misery but fell quite short. Work houses offered nothing but squalor and church groups did the best they could with the meager means they had. Paul is proposing to eliminate five whole government departments, among them, the Department of Housing and Urban Development (HUD). Do Paul's supporters realize if this department alone is abolished, millions of low income people would be thrown out into the street due to the elimination of subsidized housing? Yes, this is part of the "liberty" agenda – the freedom to die in the streets because charity organizations would be too overwhelmed to take in those kinds of numbers.

The Federal Reserve is another of Paul's favorite whipping boys and he is determined to eliminate it. I doubt very seriously that the average Paul supporter has any idea what the Fed does or the history of the central bank. In short, the Federal Reserve was created in 1913 in order to bring some stability to the banking system. It serves essentially as an instrument backing banks short term cash flow problems and set monetary policy. There was a time when panicked depositors would make runs on banks and since banks invest most of the money they have on deposit, they were vulnerable to collapse if depositors panicked. The Federal Reserve brings a measure of stability to the financial system by making loans to banks in order to keep the banks viable. Eliminating the Fed would bring greater "freedom" to the system, that is, mayhem and chaos.

There is a very fine line between Libertarianism and Anarchy. Ron Paul comes very dangerously close to anarchy with his views, some of which are not so savory. He once proposed that AIDS had been created in a U.S. government laboratory at Fort Detrick, Maryland. He blamed US foreign policy for 9/11. Paul's newsletter praised the "1,500 local militias now training to defend liberty" as "one of the most encouraging developments in America." This statement came three months before Tim McVeigh bombed the Federal building in Oklahoma City killing 168 innocent Americans. Paul's newsletters promoted all sorts of outlandish conspiracy theories of which many were racist.

A quick example: Paul alleged that "Needlin'" was a practice in which "gangs of black girls between the ages of 12 and 14" roamed the streets of New York and injected white women using possibly HIV-infected syringes. Another example was regarding the LA riots: "Order was only restored in LA when it came time for the blacks to collect their welfare checks. The 'poor' lined up at the Post Office to get their handouts (since there were no deliveries) — and then complained about slow service." What makes these allegations most egregious is that Paul denies having anything to do with what was written in his newsletters. It defies credulity that Paul had no knowledge what was being peddled in his name. If he is telling the truth then he has shown us all an incredible lack of management skills. Either way, not really Presidential material.

The other departments he wants to abolish are: Education, Commerce, Energy, and Interior. The Department of Education runs the Head Start program, the single most successful program helping disadvantaged children succeed in school. The department is also an important supplement to struggling school systems. In a time when energy is such a critical concern, eliminating the department that coordinates our energy policy is not only foolhardy but hurting our future. Come to think about it, Paul is all about bringing back the past and not even trying to look forward.

Abolishing the Department of Interior would doom our most precious heritage, our national parks system, which is the envy of the world. That proposal alone puts Paul squarely in the anarchist camp. Defunding forest management and allowing our national parks to degrade, a natural resource enjoyed by millions of Americans and a legacy for our children and grandchildren, is not only foolish but borderline unpatriotic.

What is most incomprehensible is Paul's proposal to dismantle the Department of Commerce. To his credit, he has spoken out against military engagements in favor of trade. He is a committed free trader who claims he would rather trade with countries than bomb them. Very commendable, but why eliminate the department the main function of which is to promote trade and American products abroad? The *über-conservative* Chamber of Commerce has never voiced any objection to the department so why is Paul so sanguine?

There are many more examples of Paul's over the top thinking - like eliminating consumer protections - all under the banner of liberty. If pressed he would tell you that you have the right to eat spoiled food. The next time you will be more careful when you buy. Maybe he will promote individual salmonella detection kits for consumers. It is all is so absurd and it would be funny if there weren't a sizable chunk of the population who adores this man.

The most telling aspect of Paul's liberty agenda is his unwillingness to attack Romney's predatory practices under Bain Capital. Rick Perry said it best by making a clear distinction between venture capitalism and vulture capitalism. It seems clear that Romney practiced both, but to the degree he practiced vulture capitalism he should be held accountable. There is hardly anybody on the planet who supports what the investment banks did to wreak havoc on the economy. Criticizing predatory capitalism is legitimate and it is disingenuous to pretend that attacking predatory capitalism is attacking all of capitalism.

Ron Paul has made it crystal clear that his liberty agenda includes the freedom to rape and plunder the economy. That is not real freedom. That is simply the law of the jungle – kill or be killed. Paul's career is a reflection of this "survival of the fittest" mentality. His support of armed militias, his elimination of rules to protect the public and whole departments designed to protect the most vulnerable of us points to a man who is much more than the kindly old gentleman he presents himself as. He is a wolf in sheep's clothing.

January 12, 2012

The Real Freedom Fighter

Today is a holiday celebrating the birth of Martin Luther King, Jr. It is, therefore, very appropriate that every American take time to listen to or read King's famous "I have a dream" speech. I'm not sure that's what I would call it, but history remembers it by that name. I would have preferred to call it the "Let Freedom Ring" speech.

Because the main point of his speech was about freedom. We hear a lot about freedom these days. Freedom and liberty. But after listening to King I have a feeling that the freedoms people are talking about today are not exactly what our Founding Fathers were referring to. Today, the Tea Party people are talking about freedom from paying taxes. Ron Paul's freedom is freedom from government itself. And Romney wants freedom for the jackals of society to rip into the flesh of private companies whether they are sick or healthy. The main objective is to make money in any way possible. Building it up, or tearing it down doesn't matter, as long as Mitt and his buddies get to make a ton of money.

Newt Gingrich wants freedom to teach the joy of menial labor to poor kids so they know the value of a dollar. Rick Santorum wants the freedom to tell a woman what to do with her body. He seems to know best in all cases. No exceptions, lest we freak out God Almighty. And who would know best than a politician from Pennsylvania? He has a direct line, you know. And how about good ol' boy Rick Perry? He wants the freedom to rape the land anywhere, anytime as long as there's a chance there's oil in them thar hills. And he don't want no guv'ment interference with them crazy regalations and all that there stuff.

King was talking about real freedom, that is freedom from being oppressed by government, mostly local and state. Which is when we hear politicians talking about bringing decision making back to the states it makes us wonder whether they are aware of the historical meaning of those statements. Of course they are. Those are not so subtle signals to folks who are looking for the good ole' times when you could just string up a "nigger" to the closest tree for just looking at a white woman. Nowadays, we have all these fancy courts with their complicated rules like evidence, and rights and all this stuff that just gets in the way of retribution, I mean justice.

So here's the irony for today. King who in his time was called a communist and worse by bigots had to cloak himself with the original documents of this country's foundation, the Declaration of Independence and the Constitution to find a justification for freedom. That's what happens when you let them colored folks acquire the ability to read. I mean those slave owners were right to fear literacy. Before you know it they're going to actually read the Constitution and the Bible and we will all be screwed. King's brilliant speech was all about harkening to the original promise of America. You cannot possibly get more patriotic than that. King's dream was basically that as a nation we would finally live up to that simple promise of freedom and justice for all. Something for the purveyors of fake freedom need to think carefully about.

January 16, 2012

Santorum Flunks Leadership 101

When delving into the character of a person it's the little things that tell the story. Those unscripted moments when someone does not have time to think very hard, or in the case of politicians, when they are out of earshot of their advisers, consultants, family members – anyone who would counsel prudence.

We all recognize the jerks in our lives. The person who short-changes the waitress, who steals from the collection plate, who begrudges toys for poor kids at Christmas. We all know the types. Petty little cowards who find solace in diminishing the weak, rarely standing up for what's right.

Such a man is Rick Santorum.

He spends his time preaching pious platitudes, but when it comes time to "man up" and show us that he has vestigial virtue in spite of his chosen profession, he wimps out. John McCain has many flaws but lack of leadership is not one of them. When confronted by a woman during the 2008 presidential campaign, a woman who mistakenly called Barack Obama an "Arab," McCain did not hesitate to correct her. "No ma'am," he emphatically stated. "He is decent family man citizen," McCain continued and went on to explain that he and Obama had differences of opinion but that did not make him less of an American. This is leadership.

Given a similar circumstance, Santorum did not rise to the occasion. He was confronted by a woman who not only called the President a Muslim, but said that he had no legal right to be President which is why she never refers to him as President Obama. She went further to ask why nobody was doing anything about removing him from the office he was occupying illegally. It seemed she was dumfounded that the FBI just wouldn't march into the Oval Office and carry the President away in handcuffs. Rick's response? After a short hesitation betraying his sense of panic, he lamely said that he was trying to remove him from office. And he just moved on.

Now, it can be reasonably argued that this was a minor incident that should not be used to judge Rick Santorum's leadership qualities, that it was a mere peccadillo, like when he told a group in Iowa that he didn't want their money to be given to black people. (The best part was when asked he said he didn't say "black people" he said "blah people.") Well there goes the blah people's vote. You know who you are.

This time, Santorum told reporters that it is not his job to correct people. Really? Maybe he should examine what it means to be a leader. Leaders lead. And they lead whether it is convenient or not. John McCain and other real leaders understand this. Santorum also said that the women in question was old and frail.

What? We don't expect him to take her out back and give her a beating. Just tell her the truth, for her benefit and the other knuckleheads who were there, not to mention all the people who will see this clip on TV and on the Internet. It seems that Santorum is so afraid to insult one possible voter that he lets them get away with whatever inane statement they have to offer. That is not leadership, that is cowardice.

There is no "small" matter in presidential campaigns. Everything counts. Everything is a tell about a person's character and the potential to be the leader of the free world. It should be a very high standard. I think too much was made of Rick Perry's forgetfulness, when he forgot the third element in his list during the debate. Sure it was fun when he said "oops." But that was a legitimate memory lapse. We all have one from time to time. I don't believe that was a disqualifier for high office. There were plenty of other things to disqualify Perry. This Santorum incident does not qualify as a gaffe. There was no memory lapse or incorrect pronunciation or anything like that. This was one of those telling things about a man who is incapable of showing a spine. A man who is not capable of standing up for the truth, who is incapable of showing the minimum respect toward his potential political opponent. This is not a man to be selected for the job as commander in chief of the most powerful armed forces in the world.

January 24, 2012

The Politics of
Misinformation

There is so much misinformation out there these days that it deserves a whole book. I will just limit myself to three major issues here - one from the right, one from the left and a third that is shared by most people.

1. China holds most of our debt

This is not necessarily said outright, but heavily implied by those who wish to scare the heck out of American voters. There are too many politicians still wedded to the Cold War and the current iteration of this type of thinking is making China the boogeyman. It is alleged by most elements of the right that the Chinese are our bankers. China is buying everything. China will leverage its debt to tell us what to do. China will overtake us in the next decade. The truth of the matter is that the combined U.S. debt China and Hong King hold is a mere 7.5%, hardly a commanding position. Further, although Hong Kong is technically part of China they are financially autonomous, an oasis of capitalism on the Chinese continent. The Japanese own slightly less at 6.4% and the United Kingdom owns more at

11.6%. Looks fairly balanced to me considering the relative sizes of their economies.

But the Republican claque bangs away, pretending that when elected they will be "tough" on China and not be cowed (as they accuse the President of being) by the megalith that is China. Although it is certainly true that China is huge and newly aggressive in the world, especially the Third World, the amount of debt held by the Chinese is paltry. The vast amount of American debt is owned by Americans. Surprised? You should be if you've been listening to all the propaganda out there that passes itself off as information.

2. We import most of our oil from unstable countries that are our enemies

Like most propaganda, this assertion has a germ of truth to it. We import a lot of oil from Saudi Arabia which is indeed in a volatile area. But a look at recent history tells us that when Saddam Hussein threatened Kuwait, a much smaller oil supplier, we came to Kuwait's aid in a New York minute and expelled the invaders. Now that Saddam is gone, Iraq, although still not stable, is firmly in the American sphere of influence even though Iran has a big stake there. Finally, even though Hugo Chavez is not America's best friend, he has never stopped supplying oil and refined gas through Venezuela's government owned Citgo retail outlets, long a recognized brand in America. In short, much like our debt, our oil portfolio is diversified, something a smart investment adviser would recommend.

3. President Obama is doing nothing to bring the Wall Street perpetrators to justice

Back in 2009, President Obama created a task force to investigate and prosecute financial fraud cases that led to the financial meltdown which began at the end of the Bush administration. According to Bloomberg, "The task force [formed in 2009], led by Attorney General Eric Holder, is made up of 20 federal agencies, including the Justice, Treasury, Commerce and Labor departments, 94 U.S. attorneys and state and local agencies." It turns out that prosecuting Wall Streeters is an elaborate and complicated process, involving a huge amount of manpower painstakingly reviewing thousands of documents. Since the investigation was proceeding slowly, the political pressure at the state level was such that most of the state's Attorneys General also initiated investigations on their own.

President Obama, using his leadership skills, has now also joined forces with the states with a new task force, combining the offices of all 50 state district attorneys with the Department of Justice under Attorney General Eric Holder. According to New York's Attorney General Eric Schneiderman, co-chair of the newly appointed joint task force, "In coordination with our federal partners, our office will continue its steadfast commitment to holding those responsible for the economic crisis accountable, providing meaningful relief for homeowners commensurate with the scale of the misconduct, and getting our economy moving again."

In short, the Wall Street gang responsible for the economic meltdown is hardly off the hook as the pressure mounts to get to the bottom of the origins of the crisis. It will take a substantial amount of time to wade through all the evidence which is dense, obtuse, and obscure. This is not a relatively simple case like arresting Bernie Madoff for a Ponzi scheme. There are thousands of moving parts, and the bankers in question are not being particularly cooperative. So much is at stake. What is a fabrication is the notion that the President is a prisoner of Wall Street and "doing nothing."

These are but three examples of the disinformation that is being perpetuated by the misinformed and the deliberately deceptive. There will be certainly more to come and others to bring to light as the presidential campaign continues. Stay tuned.

January 30, 2012

Deep Into the Weeds

This blog is mostly dedicated to opinion, but once in a while a few facts are good for the soul. The following is a summary of what President Obama is proposing to help homeowners. Unlike Mitt Romney who said that we should do nothing until the housing market bottoms out (and consequently more people are thrown out in the street) President Obama is proposing that the government be proactive and provide some assistance now before things get worse. People may then judge whether this President is doing something to help people or simply letting the free market take its toll.

President Obama's Plan to Help Responsible Homeowners and Heal the Housing Market

In his State of the Union address, President Obama laid out a Blueprint for an America Built to Last, calling for action to help responsible borrowers and support a housing market recovery. While the government cannot fix the housing market on its own, the President believes that responsible homeowners should not have to sit and wait for the market to hit bottom to get relief when there are measures at hand that can make a meaningful difference, including allowing these homeowners to save thousands of dollars by refinancing at today's low interest rates. That's why the President is putting forward a plan that uses the broad range of tools to help homeowners, supporting middle-class families and the economy.

Key Aspects of the President's Plan

Broad Based Refinancing to Help Responsible Borrowers Save an Average of $3,000 per Year: The President's plan will provide borrowers who are current on their payments with an opportunity to refinance and take advantage of historically low interest rates, cutting through the red tape that prevents these borrowers from saving hundreds of dollars a month and thousands of dollars a year. This plan, which is paid for by a financial fee so that it does not add a dime to the deficit, will:

Provide access to refinancing for all non-GSE borrowers who are current on their payments and meet a set of simple criteria. o Streamline the refinancing process for all GSE borrowers who are current on their loans. o Give borrowers the chance to rebuild equity through refinancing.

Homeowner Bill of Rights: The President is putting forward a single set of standards to make sure borrowers and lenders play by the same rules, including:

Access to a simple mortgage disclosure form, so borrowers understand the loans they are taking out. Full disclosure of fees and penalties. Guidelines to prevent conflicts of interest that end up hurting homeowners. Support to keep responsible families in their homes and out of foreclosure. o Protection for families against inappropriate foreclosure, including right of appeal.

First Pilot Sale to Transition Foreclosed Property into Rental Housing to Help Stabilize Neighborhoods and Improve Home Prices: The FHFA, in conjunction with Treasury and HUD, is announcing a pilot sale of foreclosed properties to be transitioned into rental housing.

Moving the Market to Provide a Full Year of Forbearance for Borrowers Looking for Work: Following the Administration's lead, major banks and the GSEs are now providing up to 12 months of forbearance to unemployed borrowers.

Pursuing a Joint Investigation into Mortgage Origination and Servicing Abuses: This effort marshals new resources to investigate misconduct that contributed to the financial crisis under the leadership of federal and state co-chairs.

Rehabilitating Neighborhoods and Reducing Foreclosures: In addition to the steps outlined above, the Administration is expanding eligibility for HAMP to reduce additional foreclosures, increasing incentives for modifications that help borrowers rebuild equity, and is proposing to put people back to work rehabilitating neighborhoods through Project Rebuild.

1. Broad Based Refinancing Plan

Millions of homeowners who are current on their mortgages and could benefit from today's low interest rates face substantial barriers to refinancing through no fault of their own. Sometimes homeowners with good credit and clean payment histories are rejected because their mortgages are underwater. In other cases, they are rejected because the banks are worried that they will be left taking losses, even where Fannie Mae or Freddie Mac insure these new mortgages. In the end, these responsible homeowners are stuck paying higher interest rates, costing them thousands of dollars a year.

To address this challenge, the President worked with housing regulators this fall to take action without Congress to make millions of Americans eligible for lower interest rates. However, there are still millions of responsible Americans who continue to face steep barriers to low-cost, streamlined refinancing. So the President is now calling on Congress to open up opportunities to refinancing for responsible borrowers who are current on their payments.

Under the proposal, borrowers with loans insured by Fannie Mae or Freddie Mac (i.e. GSE-insured loans) will have access to streamlined refinancing through the GSEs. Borrowers with standard non-GSE loans will have access to refinancing through a new program run through the FHA. For responsible borrowers, there will be no more barriers and no more excuses.

Key components of the President's plan include:

Providing Non-GSE Borrowers Access to Simple, Low-Cost Refinancing: President Obama is calling on Congress to pass legislation to establish a streamlined refinancing program. The refinancing program will be open to all non-GSE borrowers with standard (non-jumbo) loans who have been keeping up with their mortgage payments. The program will be operated through the FHA.

Simple and straightforward eligibility criteria: Any borrower with a loan that is not currently guaranteed by the GSEs can qualify if they meet the following criteria:

They are current on their mortgage: Borrowers will need to have been current on their loan for the past 6 months and have missed no more than one payment in the 6 months prior. · They meet a minimum credit score. Borrowers must have a current FICO score of 580 to be eligible. Approximately 9 in 10 borrowers have a credit score adequate to meet that requirement. They have a loan that is no larger than the current FHA conforming loan limits in their area: Currently, FHA limits vary geographically with the median area home price – set at $271,050 in lowest cost areas and as high as $729,750 in the highest cost areas The loan they are refinancing is for a single family, owner-occupied principal residence. This will ensure that the program is focused on responsible homeowners trying to stay in their homes.

Streamlined application process: Borrowers will apply through a streamlined process designed to make it simpler and less expensive for borrowers and lenders to refinance. Borrowers will not be required to submit a new appraisal or tax return. To determine a borrower's eligibility, a lender need only confirm that the borrower is employed. (Those who are not employed may still be eligible if they meet the other requirements and present limited credit risk. However, a lender will need to perform a full underwriting of these borrowers to determine whether they are a good fit for the program.)

Program parameters to reduce program cost: The President's plan includes additional steps to reduce program costs, including:

Establishing loan-to-value limits for these loans. The Administration will work with Congress to establish risk-mitigation measures which could include requiring lenders interested in refinancing deeply underwater loans (e.g. greater than 140 LTV) to write down the balance of these loans before they qualify. This would reduce the risk associated with the program and relieve the strain of negative equity on the borrower.

Creating a separate fund for new streamlined refinancing program. This will help the FHA better track and manage the risk involved and ensure that it has no effect on the operation of the existing Mutual Mortgage Insurance (MMI) fund.

EXAMPLE: How Refinancing Can Benefit a Borrower With a Non-GSE Loan

A borrower has a non-GSE mortgage originated in 2005 with a 6 percent rate and an initial balance of $300,000 – resulting in monthly payments of about $1,800. The outstanding balance is now about $272,000 and the borrower's home is now worth $225,000, leaving the borrower underwater (with a loan-to-value ratio of about 120%). Though the borrower has been paying his mortgage on time, he cannot refinance at today's historically low rates. Under the President's legislative plan, the borrower would be eligible to refinance into a 4.25% percent 30-year loan, which would reduce monthly payments by about $460 a month.

Refinancing Plan Will Be Fully Paid For By a Portion of Fee on Largest Financial Institutions: The Administration estimates the cost of its refinancing plan will be in the range of $5 to $10 billion, depending on exact parameters and take-up. This cost will be fully offset by using a portion of the President's proposed Financial Crisis Responsibility Fee, which imposes a fee on the largest financial institutions based on their size and the riskiness of their activities – ensuring that the program does not add a dime to the deficit.

Fully Streamlining Refinancing for All GSE Borrowers: The Administration has worked with the FHFA to streamline the GSEs' refinancing program for all responsible, current GSE borrowers. The FHFA has made important progress to-date, including eliminating the restriction on allowing deeply underwater borrowers to access refinancing, lowering fees associated with refinancing, and making it easier to access refinancing with lower closing costs.

To build on this progress, the Administration is calling on Congress to enact additional changes that will benefit homeowners and save taxpayers money by reducing the number of defaults on GSE loans. We believe these steps are within the existing authority of the FHFA. However, to date, the GSEs have not acted, so the Administration is calling on Congress to do what is in the taxpayer's interest, by:

a. Eliminating appraisal costs for all borrowers: Borrowers who happen to live in communities without a significant number of recent home sales often have to get a manual appraisal to determine whether they are eligible for refinancing into a GSE guaranteed loan, even under the HARP program. Under the Administration's proposal, the GSEs would be directed to use mark-to-market accounting or other alternatives to manual appraisals for any loans for which the loan-to-value cannot be determined with the GSE's Automated Valuation Model. This will eliminate a significant barrier that will reduce cost and time for borrowers and lenders alike.

b. Increasing competition so borrowers get the best possible deal: Today, lenders looking to compete with the current servicer of a borrower's loan for that borrower's refinancing business continue to face barriers to participating in HARP. This lack of competition means higher prices and less favorable terms for the borrower. The President's legislative plan would direct the GSEs to require the same streamlined underwriting for new servicers as they do for current servicers, leveling the playing field and unlocking competition between banks for borrowers' business.

c. Extending streamlined refinancing for all GSE borrowers: The President's plan would extend these steps to streamline refinancing for homeowners to all GSE borrowers. Those who have significant equity in their home – and thus present less credit risk – should benefit fully from all streamlining, including lower fees and fewer barriers. This will allow more borrowers to take advantage of a program that provides streamlined, low-cost access to today's low interest rates – and make it easier and more automatic for servicers to market and promote this program for all GSE borrowers.

Giving Borrowers the Chance to Rebuild Equity in their Homes Through Refinancing: All underwater borrowers who decide to participate in either HARP or the refinancing program through the FHA outlined above will have a choice: they can take the benefit of the reduced interest rate in the form of lower monthly payments, or they can apply that savings to rebuilding equity in their homes. The latter course, when combined with a shorter loan term of 20 years, will give the majority of underwater borrowers the chance to get back above water within five years, or less.

To encourage borrowers to make the decision to rebuild equity in their homes, we are proposing that the legislation provide for the GSEs and FHA to cover the closing costs of borrowers who chose this option – a benefit averaging about $3,000 per homeowner. To be eligible, a participant in either program must agree to refinance into a loan with a no more than 20 year term with monthly payments roughly equal to those they make under their current loan. For those who agree to these terms, the lender will receive payment for all closing costs directly from the GSEs or the FHA, depending on the entity involved.

EXAMPLE: *How Rebuilding Equity Can Benefit a Borrower*

A borrower has a 6.5 percent $214,000 30-year mortgage ori-ginated in 2006. It now has an outstanding balance of $200,000, but the house is worth $160,000 (a loan-to-value ratio of 125). The monthly payment on this mortgage is $1,350.

While this borrower is responsibly paying her monthly mortgage, she is locked out of refinancing.

By refinancing into a 4.25 percent 30-year mortgage loan, this borrower will reduce her monthly payment by $370. However, after five years her mortgage balance will remain at $182,000.

Under the rebuilding equity program, the borrower would refinance into a 20-year mortgage at 3.75 percent and commit her monthly savings to paying down principal. After five years, her mortgage balance would decline to $152,000, bringing the borrower above water.

If the borrower took this option, the GSEs or FHA would also cover her closing costs – potentially saving her about $3,000.

Streamlined Refinancing for Rural America: The Agriculture Department, which supports mortgage financing for thousands of rural families a year, is taking steps to further streamline its USDA-to-USDA refinancing program. This program is designed to provide those who currently have loans insured by the Department of Agriculture with a low-cost, streamlined process for refinancing into today's low rates. The Administration is announcing that the Agriculture Department will further streamline this program by eliminating the requirement for a new appraisal, a new credit report and other documentation normally required in a refinancing. To be eligible, a borrower need only demonstrate that he or she has been current on their loan.

Streamlined Refinancing for FHA Borrowers: Like the Agriculture Department, the Federal Housing Authority is taking steps to make it easier for borrowers with loans insured by their agency to obtain access to low-cost, streamlined refinancing. The current FHA-to-FHA streamlined refinance program allows FHA borrowers who are current on their mortgage to refinance into a new FHA-insured loan at today's lower interest rates without requiring a full re-underwrite of the loan, thereby providing a simple way for borrowers to reduce their mortgage payments.

However, some borrowers who would be eligible for low-cost refinancing through this program are being denied by lenders reticent to make loans that may compromise their status as FHA-approved lenders. To resolve this issue, the FHA is removing these loans from their "Compare Ratio", the process by which the performance of these lenders is reviewed. This will open the program up to many more families with FHA-insured loans.

2. Homeowner Bill of Rights

EXAMPLE: How Rebuilding Equity Can Benefit a Borrower:

The Administration believes that the mortgage servicing system is badly broken and would benefit from a single set of strong federal standards As we have learned over the past few years, the nation is not well served by the inconsistent patchwork of standards in place today, which fails to provide the needed support for both homeowners and investors. The Administration believes that there should be one set of rules that borrowers and lenders alike can follow. A fair set of rules will allow lenders to be transparent about options and allow borrowers to meet their responsibilities to understand the terms of their commitments.

The Administration will therefore work closely with regulators, Congress and stakeholders to create a more robust and comprehensive set of rules that better serves borrowers, investors, and the overall housing market. These rules will be driven by the following set of core principles:

Simple, Easy to Understand Mortgage Forms: Every prospective homeowner should have access to clear, straightforward forms that help inform rather than confuse them when making what is for most families their most consequential financial purchase. To help fulfill this objective, the Consumer Financial Protection Bureau (CFPB) is in the process of developing a simple mortgage disclosure form to be used in all home loans, replacing overlapping and complex forms that include hidden clauses and opaque terms that families cannot understand.

No Hidden Fees and Penalties: Servicers must disclose to homeowners all known fees and penalties in a timely manner and in understandable language, with any changes disclosed before they go into effect.

No Conflicts of Interest: Servicers and investors must implement standards that minimize conflicts of interest and facilitate coordination and communication, including those between multiple investors and junior lien holders, such that loss mitigation efforts are not hindered for borrowers.

Assistance For At-Risk Homeowners:

Early Intervention: Servicers must make reasonable efforts to contact every homeowner who has either demonstrated hardship or fallen delinquent and provide them with a comprehensive set of options to help them avoid foreclosure. Every such homeowner must be given a reasonable time to apply for a modification.

Continuity of Contact: Servicers must provide all homeowners who have requested assistance or fallen delinquent on their mortgage with access to a customer service employee with 1) a complete record of previous communications with that homeowner; 2) access to all documentation and payments submitted by the homeowner; and 3) access to personnel with decision-making authority on loss mitigation options.

Time and Options to Avoid Foreclosure: Servicers must not initiate a foreclosure action unless they are unable to establish contact with the homeowner after reasonable efforts, or the homeowner has shown a clear inability or lack of interest in pursuing alternatives to foreclosure. Any foreclosure action already under way must stop prior to sale once the servicer has received the required documentation and cannot be restarted unless and until the homeowner fails to complete an application for a modification within a reasonable period, their application for a modification has been denied or the homeowner fails to comply with the terms of the modification received.

Safeguards Against Inappropriate Foreclosure

Right of Appeal: Servicers must explain to all homeowners any decision to take action based on a failure by the homeowner to meet their payment obligations and provide a reasonable opportunity to appeal that decision in a formal review process.

Certification of Proper Process: Prior to a foreclosure sale, servicers must certify in writing to the foreclosure attorney or trustee that appropriate loss mitigation alternatives have been considered and that proceeding to foreclosure sale is consistent with applicable law. A copy of this certification must be provided to the borrower.

The agencies of the executive branch with oversight or other authority over servicing practices –the FHA, the USDA, the VA, and Treasury, through the HAMP program – will each take the steps needed in the coming months to implement rules for their programs that are consistent with these standards.

3. Announcement of Initial Pilot Sale in Initiative to Transition Real Estate Owned (REO) Property to Rental Housing to Stabilize Neighborhoods and Improve Housing Prices

When there are vacant and foreclosed homes in neighborhoods, it undermines home prices and stalls the housing recovery. As part of the Administration's effort to help lay the foundation for a stronger housing recovery, the Department of Treasury and HUD have been working with the FHFA on a strategy to transition REO properties into rental housing. Repurposing foreclosed and vacant homes will reduce the inventory of unsold homes, help stabilize housing prices, support neighborhoods, and provide sustainable rental housing for American families.

Today, the FHFA is announcing the first major pilot sale of foreclosed properties into rental housing. This marks the first of a series of steps that the FHFA and the Administration will take to develop a smart national program to help manage REO properties, easing the pressure of these distressed properties on communities and the housing market.

4. Moving the Market to Provide a Full Year of Forbearance for Borrowers Looking for Work

Last summer, the Administration announced that it was extending the minimum forbearance period that unemployed borrowers in FHA and HAMP would receive on their mortgages to a full year, up from four months in FHA and three months in HAMP. This forbearance period allows borrowers to stay in their homes while they look for jobs, which gives these families a better chance of avoiding default and helps the housing market by reducing the number of foreclosures. Extending this period makes good economic sense as the time it takes the average unemployed American to find work has grown through the course of the housing crisis: nearly 60 percent of unemployed Americans are now out of work for more than four months.

These extensions went into effect for HAMP and the FHA in October. Today the Administration is announcing that the market has followed our lead, finally giving millions of families the time needed to find work before going into default.

12-Month Forbearance for Mortgages Owned by the GSEs: Fannie Mae and Freddie Mac have both announced that lenders servicing their loans can provide up to a year of forbearance for unemployed borrowers, up from 3 months. Between them, Fannie and Freddie cover nearly half of the market, so this alone will extend the relief available for a considerable portion of the nation's unemployed homeowners.

Move by Major Servicers to Use 12-Month Forbearance as Default Approach: Key servicers have also followed the Administration's lead in extending forbearance for the unemployed to a year. Wells Fargo and Bank of America, two of the nation's largest lenders, have begun to offer this longer period to customers whose loans they hold on their own books, recognizing that it is not just helpful for these struggling families, but it makes good economic sense for their lenders as well.

A New Industry Norm: With these steps, the industry is gradually moving to a norm of providing 12 months of forbearance for those looking for work. This is a significant shift worthy of note, as only a few months ago unemployed borrowers simply were not being given a fighting chance to find work before being faced with the added burden of a monthly mortgage payment.

5. Joint Investigation into Mortgage Origination and Servicing Abuses

The Department of Justice, the Department of Housing and Urban Development, the Securities and Exchange Commission and state Attorneys General have formed a Residential Mortgage-Backed Securities Working Group under President Obama's Financial Fraud Enforcement Task Force that will be responsible for investigating misconduct contributing to the financial crisis through the pooling and sale of residential mortgage-backed securities. The Department of Justice has announced that this working group will consist of at least 55 DOJ attorneys, analysts, agents and investigators from around the country, joining existing state and federal resources investigating similar misconduct under those authorities.

The working group will be co-chaired by senior officials at the Department of Justice and SEC, including Lanny Breuer, Assistant Attorney General, Criminal Division, DOJ; Robert Khuzami, Director of Enforcement, SEC; John Walsh, U.S. Attorney, District of Colorado; and Tony West, Assistant Attorney General, Civil Division, DOJ. The working group will also be co-chaired by New York Attorney General Schneiderman, who will lead the effort from the state level. Other state Attorneys General have been and will be joining this effort.

6. Putting People Back to Work Rehabilitating Homes, Businesses and Communities Through Project Rebuild

Consistent with a proposal he first put forward in the American Jobs Act, the President will propose in his Budget to invest $15 billion in a national effort to put construction workers on the job rehabilitating and refurbishing hundreds of thousands of vacant and foreclosed homes and businesses. Building on proven approaches to stabilizing neighborhoods with high concentrations of foreclosures – including those piloted through the Neighborhood Stabilization Program – Project Rebuild will bring in expertise and capital from the private sector, focus on commercial and residential property improvements, and expand innovative property solutions like land banks.

In addition, the Budget will provide $1 billion in mandatory funding in 2013 for the Housing Trust Fund to finance the development, rehabilitation and preservation of affordable housing for extremely low income families. These approaches will not only create construction jobs but will help reduce blight and crime and stabilize housing prices in areas hardest hit by the housing crisis.

7. Expanding HAMP Eligibility to Reduce Additional Foreclosures and Help Stabilize Neighborhoods

To date, the Home Affordable Mortgage Program (HAMP) has helped more than 900,000 families permanently modify their loans, providing them with savings of about $500 a month on average. Combined with measures taken by the FHA and private sector modifications, public and private efforts have helped more than 4.6 million Americans get mortgage aid to prevent avoidable foreclosures. Along with extending the HAMP program by one year to December 31, 2013, the Administration is expanding the eligibility for the program so that it reaches a broader pool of distressed borrowers. Additional borrowers will now have an opportunity to receive modification assistance that provides the same homeowner protections and clear rules for servicers established by HAMP. This includes:

Ensuring that Borrowers Struggling to Make Ends Meet Because of Debt Beyond Their Mortgage Can Participate in the Program: To date, if a borrower's first-lien mortgage debt-to-income ratio is below 31% they are ineligible for a HAMP modification. Yet many homeowners who have an affordable first mortgage payment – below that 31% threshold – still struggle beneath the weight of other debt such as second liens and medical bills. Therefore, we are expanding the program to those who struggle with this secondary debt by offering an alternative evaluation opportunity with more flexible debt-to-income criteria.

Preventing Additional Foreclosures to Support Renters and Stabilize Communities: We will also expand eligibility to include properties that are currently occupied by a tenant or which the borrower intends to rent. This will provide critical relief to both renters and those who rent their homes, while further stabilizing communities from the blight of vacant and foreclosed properties. Single-family homes are an important source of affordable rental housing, and foreclosure of non-owner occupied homes has disproportionate negative effects on low-and moderate-income renters.

8. Increasing Incentives for Modifications that Help Borrowers Rebuild Equity

Currently, HAMP includes an option for servicers to provide homeowners with a modification that includes a write-down of the borrower's principal balance when a borrower owes significantly more on their mortgage than their home is worth. These principal reduction modifications help both reduce a borrower's monthly payment and rebuild equity in their homes. While not appropriate in all circumstances, principal reduction modifications are an important tool in the overall effort to help homeowners achieve affordable and sustainable mortgages. To further encourage investors to consider or expand use of principal reduction modifications, the Administration will:

Triple the Incentives Provided to Encourage the Reduction of Principal for Underwater Borrowers: To date, the owner of a loan that qualifies for HAMP receives between 6 and 21 cents on the dollar to write down principal on that loan, depending on the degree of change in the loan-to-value ratio. To increase the amount of principal that is written down, Treasury will triple those incentives, paying from 18 to 63 cents on the dollar.

Offer Principal Reduction Incentives for Loans Insured or Owned by the GSEs: HAMP borrowers who have loans owned or guaranteed by Fannie Mae or Freddie Mac do not currently benefit from principal reduction loan modifications. To encourage the GSEs to offer this assistance to its underwater borrowers, Treasury has notified the GSE's regulator, FHFA, that it will pay principal reduction incentives to Fannie Mae or Freddie Mac if they allow servicers to forgive principal in conjunction with a HAMP modification.

[Source: HUD]

February 1, 2012

Moscow's Blunder

In the good old days of the Cold War, the USSR's secret weapon was consistent support of the Third World. The Russians could be counted on to block any move by the United States and its allies to either help Israel or to move against any of the dozens of Third World dictators, especially the left-wing ones like Cuba. In those days the Russians were the king makers in the United Nations. That is why even relatively moderate regimes like Egypt and India were pro-Russian. And the Russians milked it to the max. They promoted themselves as the defenders of the downtrodden against the capitalist leviathan that was the United States of America. In the last few days, however, their reputation in the Third World has suffered a devastating blow.

Even when the vast Soviet empire crumbled and Communism retreated to its current diminutive dimension, the newly formed "democratic" Russian federation still tried to continue a foreign policy of defending the infelicitous. America was still seen with jaundiced eyes by a resentful nation that considered itself every bit its equal. Reduced to a second tier power, the Russian oligarchs still rarely miss an opportunity to flex whatever muscles they have left. Their precious veto power in the UN is still one of their last remaining tools.

Among American conservatives, however, the UN is a sordid organization. Never mind that the UN was an invention born of American idealism, with its headquarters in New York. That matters little to the people who resent the one country, one vote system. How dare an insignificant country like Zambia have the same vote as the mighty US? These people conveniently forget that in their own country, under the magnificent Constitution they claim to revere, that Bill Gates has the same vote as Joe the Plumber. (I suppose logic was never their strong suit.) Conservatives hate the fact that the despised Cold War rivals, the dastardly Russians, still have veto power. No wonder the conservatives, those professional patriots, think the UN is irrelevant. It's pretty much the same reason they think President Obama is immaterial. They don't support anything they can't control. The UN is not "ours." We created it as our contribution to world peace, where there could be a forum where the world could have the opportunity to discuss problems without violence. Not a bad goal.

So it's not perfect.

Our Congress was created by none other than our Founding Fathers and we have seen over the year that it is also far from perfect, but until we devise another system that's what we have and we should make the best of it.

The Russians made a huge mistake in vetoing the resolution proposed by the Arab League as a solution for the turmoil in Syria. The Arab League has asked Syrian President Assad to turn over the country to a democratic process, whereby the people of Syria could elect their own leaders. The League received the endorsement of the United States and its allies therefore putting us squarely on their side.

The Russians' shortsightedness in supporting their crony Assad will backfire because with this veto they finally lost the high ground of support for the Third World, especially the Muslim world which is considerable, particularly in Africa. The Chinese, who also have huge stakes in Africa, made the same mistake. Apparently old habits die hard. Both the Chinese and the Russians are so used to vetoing everything Americans support that they didn't notice that this time, the Americans are on the right side of history. The Russian veto will complicate their relationships with the Muslim world and in a seemingly knee jerk response the Chinese followed suit. They are counting on Assad to prevail in Syria, but it doesn't look very good for him. Even if he survives he will be a lame duck at best. Not the kind of ally you need in this volatile area.

The Obama administration, led by Secretary Clinton got it right, and the Russians (and the Chinese) blundered.

February 7, 2012

Religion and Politics

"Congress shall make no law respecting an establishment of religion, or prohibiting the free exercise thereof;"

These are the exact words in the first amendment of the Constitution. This simple clause has been interpreted in many ways, but a few things seem very clear. First, it is clear that Congress cannot favor any particular religion over another or impose any religion on the Nation. And second, it also seems clear that Congress cannot pass any laws preventing people's religious freedom. I hope that most Americans would agree with these two fundamental points.

Notice that the first amendment says nothing about religions being able to impose their religion on non-practitioners. The Catholics and the Jews are particularly vulnerable on this point because of their notorious inability to impose all their rules on their own people. There are many Jews who do not obey the kosher laws, for example. Jews divide themselves into many groups – Orthodox (Haredi, Hasidic, Modern), Conservative, Reform, Karaite, Reconstructionist, Renewal, Humanistic – precisely to accommodate the diversity of opinion on traditional observances. Catholic women overwhelmingly practice birth control even though it is against Church dogma, The Church has failed miserably to equate contraception with abortion.

The Komen foundation has found out the hard way that injecting religious politics into their charity work is not acceptable to the public, especially women. The sad part is the Komen foundation had a stellar reputation as the premiere organization fighting breast cancer. They had partnerships with many legitimate institutions, from Planned Parenthood to the NFL. They were indeed mainstream and were able to bring breast cancer to the Nation's attention. And then some of the people in the leadership at Komen decided to play politics. The obviously partisan investigation in Congress gave them the opening to drop Planned Parenthood, an organization despised by the religious right. The move was an unmistakeable attempt to link breast cancer with abortion where none exists.

The Komen foundation made the mistake of thinking that women would accept dropping Planned Parenthood from their breast cancer network due to the perception by some that Planned Parenthood is all about abortion. Notoriously, Senator Jon Kyle of Arizona had previously stated on the floor of the Senate that Planned Parenthood's work was "over 90%" about abortion, when in reality the number is around 3%. To add insult to injury, the following day Kyl's office issued the laughable statement that "his remark was not intended to be a factual statement." It is not surprising that due to so much misinformation [see blog entry "The Politics of Misinformation"] that some people are confused about what and whom to believe.

The flap over Planned Parenthood was a self-inflicted wound by Komen. All they had to do was stick to their mandate and everything would have been fine. But politics reared its ugly head and not only did Komen reverse itself, but this has really damaged their reputation unnecessarily. The work of the Komen Foundation is important but they have only themselves to blame for the backlash. Let's hope they come to their senses and keep politics out of their good work going forward.

Apparently having learned little from the Komen Foundation flap, Catholic Bishops are at it again. They just can't resist grabbing headlines and jumping into the political fray. The idea of making contraception a part of basic health care being an attack on religious freedom is absurd. Nobody is suggesting that women should be forced to use contraception against their will or doctors forced to prescribe them against their will. The irony, of course, is that 98% of Catholic women have used contraception at least at one point in their lives. Contraception is one Church mandate that is routinely ignored by most Catholics. So for the Bishops to make contraception the center piece of the President's curtailment of religious liberty, while a nice slogan for Republicans to bash Obama with, will backfire among the non-partisan middle, not to mention fire up women of all persuasions. The idea that people of conscience should not be required to pay for things they don't believe in is absurd in a democracy. Freedom to practice your religion of choice is not a mandate to impose your morality on others. The Quakers have always been morally opposed to wars of all kinds but they are not exempt from paying taxes that support the military. I don't have any children in my local schools yet I am forced to pay taxes supporting schools. I don't complain about that. That is my contribution to my community. People routinely are required to pay for things they don't need or don't believe in whether a matter of conscience or religion.

What the Bishops are saying, however, is that they have the right to impose their morality on people who don't believe as they do. That is not freedom. Your freedom ends when it impacts upon other people's freedom. Which is why we are not "free" to throw a rock through our neighbor's window. The Catholic Bishops have injected themselves into the Presidential campaign on purpose, to highlight their issues. By doing so they have enabled all the conservatives to jump on the "freedom" bandwagon and pretend that the President is somehow anti-religious and must be stopped. This is demagoguery at its worse. The Bishops had every opportunity to quietly bring up their concerns to the President, but they chose to play the political game, incidentally violating their own Church mandate concerning political action in the process.

Politics and religion, as so adroitly addressed by our Founding Fathers in the Constitution, are not a healthy mix. As Jesus himself said in Matthew 22:21 Ἀπόδοτε οὖν τὰ Καίσαρος Καίσαρι καὶ τὰ τοῦ Θεοῦ τῷ Θεῷ ("Render unto Caesar the things which are Caesar's, and unto God the things that are God's.") Couldn't have said it better myself.

February 9, 2012

The President's Budget

Before the pundits and the politicians declare the President's budget dead, or irrelevant or something other than serious policy, it might be interesting to review the highlights of the budget that was just released by the President and sent to Congress for its consideration. People should be able to evaluate for themselves whether this is a reasonable blueprint for our situation at this juncture in our history. The following are the major highlights.

◆ In the Budget Control Act, both parties in Congress and the President agreed to tight spending caps that reduce discretionary spending by $1 trillion over 10 years. This budget reflects that decision. Thus, for all the priority areas we are investing in, difficult trade-offs had to be made to meet these very tight caps. Discretionary spending is reduced from 8.7 percent of GDP in 2011 to 5.0 percent in 2022.

◆ Including the $1 trillion in discretionary cuts, the Budget includes more than $4 trillion in balanced, deficit reduction so that, by 2018, we cut the deficit to less than 3 percent of GDP, stabilize the debt-to-GDP ratio, and achieve primary balance.

◆ For every $1 in new revenue from those making more than $250,000 per year and from closing corporate loopholes, the

Budget has $2.50 in spending cuts including the deficit reduction enacted over the last year.

◆ 2012 Projected Deficit: $1.33 trillion, 8.5 percent of GDP; 2013 Projected Deficit: $901 billion, 5.5 percent of GDP; 2018 Projected Deficit: $575 billion, 2.7 percent of GDP; 2022 Projected Deficit: $704 billion, 2.8 percent of GDP.

JUMPSTART JOB CREATION

◆ More than $350 billion in short-term measures for job growth starting in 2012, including many planks of the American Jobs Act that we continue to call on Congress to enact plus some new job creation initiatives. They include:

◆ Extension of the payroll tax cut and unemployment insurance benefits for rest of 2012.

◆ An upfront investment of $50 billion from the surface transportation reauthorization bill for roads, rails, and runways to create thousands of quality jobs in the short term.

◆ Continuing to allow businesses to write-off the full amount of new investments.

◆ $30 billion to modernize at least 35,000 schools and $30 billion to help states and localities retain and hire teachers and first responders.

◆ Project Rebuild, a series of policies to help connect Americans looking for work in distressed communities with the work needed to re-purpose residential and commercial properties, creating jobs and stabilizing neighborhoods.

◆ A new tax credit for this year focused on small businesses and that gives businesses that add jobs and wages a tax cut equal to 10 percent of wages added up to $500,000.

EDUCATION AND SKILLS
FOR AMERICAN WORKERS

◆ $850 million for Race to the Top, which implements systemic education reforms in five critical areas, including early learning and care. The Budget also provides $300 million in new resources to improve child care quality and prepare children for success in school.

◆ A new $5 billion competitive program that will challenge states and districts to work with their teachers and unions to attract, prepare, and reward great teachers to help students learn.

◆ Make college more affordable and help achieve the President's goal of the U.S. leading the world in college graduates by 2020:

◆ Sustains the maximum Pell Grant award through the 2014-2015 award year.

◆ A one-year measure to prevent student loan interest rates from doubling this summer and doubles the number of work-study jobs.

◆ New reforms to help address rising costs by shifting some Federal aid away from colleges that fail to keep net tuition down and by providing incentives for States and colleges to keep costs under control.

◆ Makes permanent the American Opportunity Tax Credit (AOTC) -- a partially refundable tax credit worth up to $10,000 per student over four years of college. AOTC helps more than 9 million students and their families afford the cost of college.

◆ Supports State and community college partnerships with businesses to build the skills of American workers, and creates a Pathways Back to Work Fund, which will support summer and year-round jobs for low-income youth, and will help connect the long-term unemployed and low-income adults to subsidized employment and work-based training opportunities.

AMERICAN INNOVATION
AND MANUFACTURING

◆ $140.8 billion for R&D overall; increase the level of investment in non-defense R&D by 5 percent from the 2012 level, even as overall budgets decline; maintains the President's commitment to double the budgets of three key basic research agencies (National Science Foundation, Department of Energy's Office of Science, and National Institute of Standards and Technology Laboratories); expands and makes permanent the R&D tax credit.

◆ $2.2 billion for advanced manufacturing R&D, a 19 percent increase over 2012.

◆ Provides tax incentives for manufacturers who create jobs here at home and doubles the deduction for advanced manufacturing; ends tax deductions for shipping jobs overseas; and establishes a Manufacturing Communities Tax Credit to encourage investment in communities affected by job loss.

◆   Level funding for biomedical research at NIH ($30.7 billion); and to get more out of the money, proposes new grant management policies to increase the number of new research grants by 7 percent.

◆   Supports the goals of: putting one million electric vehicles on the road by 2015; doubling share of electricity from clean energy sources by 2035; and reducing buildings' energy use by 20 percent by 2020.

◆   Elimination of 12 tax breaks to oil, gas, and coal companies will raise $41 billion over 10 years.

BUILD AMERICA: A 21ST CENTURY INFRASTRUCTURE

◆   A six-year, $476 billion surface transportation reauthorization bill – expanded to included inter-city passenger rail – to create thousands of new jobs and modernize a critical foundation of our economic growth.

◆   Fully paid for through current user-financed mechanisms and part of the savings from ending the war in Iraq and winding down operations in Afghanistan.

◆   Get the most out of taxpayer dollars through: a "fix-it first" policy, consolidation of 55 duplicative highway programs into five, and using a Race to the Top-style competition to bring about reform.

◆　　　　National Infrastructure Bank to fund projects of national importance.

◆　　　　Builds a next-generation, wireless broadband network for public safety users.

◆　　　　Plan is fully paid for, and the sale of spectrum provides nearly $21 billion for deficit reduction.

AMERICAN VALUES: EVERYONE PAYS THEIR FAIR SHARE

◆　　　　Calls for individual tax reform that: cuts the deficit by $1.5 trillion, including the expiration of the high-income 2001 and 2003 tax cuts; simplifies the tax code, lowers tax rates, and protects progressivity; eliminates inefficient and unfair tax breaks for millionaires while making all tax breaks at least as good for the middle class as for the wealthy; and observes the Buffett Rule that no household making more than $1 million a year pays less than 30 percent of their income in taxes.

◆　　　　Scores of cuts and consolidations including more than $7.5 billion in administrative savings.

◆　　　　Financial Crisis Responsibility Fee on largest financial institutions to fully compensate taxpayers for their extraordinary support. Raises $61 billion over 10 years and is intended to offset cost of TARP and the President's mortgage refinancing program.

◆   More than $360 billion in savings to Medicare, Medicaid, and other health programs over 10 years to make these programs more effective and efficient and move our health system to one that rewards high-quality medicine.

◆ $278 billion in non-health mandatory savings through reforms in areas such as: agriculture subsidies and direct payments, federal civilian worker retirement, and the PBGC.

◆   Implements the new defense strategy to spend $487 billion less in the Department of Defense's base budget than was planned in last year's Budget. Overall defense budget, including overseas contingency operations, is 5 percent below last year's enacted level.

[source: OMB]

February 14, 2012

The Last Gasps
of Dinosaurs

I know this may offend many of my female friends but contraception is not exclusively a woman's issue. Granted, women directly feel the consequences of an unplanned child. After all, they are the ones who get pregnant. Still, birth control is a people issue. Men, are usually involved (in spite of advances in medicine) in some way or another.

Men have a strong stake in birth control, whether they are married, single, promiscuous or monogamous. What, there are monogamous men? Yes, Virginia they do exist. But all kidding aside, the idea that contraception is exclusively a woman's issue is just not true.

So when people say that a prude like Rick Santorum is alienating women, yes it is true, but he is also alienating a big chunk of sexually active (and sexually wannabe active) men. Maybe the good bishops of the Catholic Church may not be aware of this, but men young and old fantasize of having sex with pretty much every woman they come in contact with. Fortunately, they don't always act upon these desires, but the desire is typically there. Trust me. Of course there are some of us of the male gender who are capable of resisting the temptation, much like there are women who are capable of resisting grabbing that last piece of Belgian chocolate left on the cocktail party tray.

The recent "debate" about contraception sounds like only women practice it. Has anybody heard of condoms? According to the CDC over 10 billion condoms were sold in 2005. Furthermore, condoms are not just for birth control. They are also protection from the spread of sexually transmitted diseases, an important consideration since female birth control doesn't address this issue. So men are kind of important in discussing sex that might or might not lead to procreation.

Here's the rub. All this talk of contraception, or religious "freedom" is really about sex. I could make a joke about the bishops not being concerned about contraception because their interest in sex is in creating as many Catholics as possible and abusing children, but I won't. That would be in poor taste. I will say, however, that the Church's problem is with sex without the explicit intention of creating a new human being, so contraception is rather irrelevant to them. Rick Santorum has clearly stated his belief that sex is "wrong" if not done to procreate. That's nice. He has the right to believe as he wishes. What he does not have the right to do is shove his morality down everybody else's throat. What is astounding is that Republicans in Congress have jumped on this anti-sex, anti-contraception bandwagon.

In the case of the Congressmen, I doubt their new found distaste for contraception is anything more than a thinly disguised attack on that dastardly plan, that monstrosity they call "Obamacare". They have been trying to derail the Affordable Health Care Act (its real name) since its inception. And they have personalized it to make it clear who they want to get rid of in the bargain.

I suspect that the GOP is not really afraid of what health care will do to the nation. All this talk of "death panels" and "government takeover" and "religious liberty" are really cover stories masking their real fear. Republicans fear that once Americans find out what is in health care reform, they will actually **like** it. Already, Americans have had a taste of what is to come. Free yearly checkups have already popped up on many people's insurance cards. Also, keeping your kids on the family plan until they're 26 doesn't seem to create much anxiety among most Americans as there are no massive demonstrations against this type of "government intrusion". And now, free birth control for women. I didn't notice many women complaining about that. Only old fuddy duddy men who try to claim that their rights as men of conscience are being trampled upon if women have access to free birth control. Yes, there is fear in the minds of zealots, partisans who are increasing irrelevant in the public square. Their sway over public opinion is waning. As the Bard so aptly put it:

Come senators, congressmen
Please heed the call
Don't stand in the doorway
Don't block up the hall
For he that gets hurt
Will be he who has stalled
There's a battle outside
And it is ragin'

It'll soon shake your windows
And rattle your walls
For the times they are a-changin'.

Bob Dylan

The fear of change is what drives the retrograde, the traditionalist, the reactionary. The GOP is losing its grip on the American agenda and they are dangerous like a wild animal is dangerous when it is wounded. They are desperately attacking the President because he is reflective of America's current values, as their own values are becoming passé. They draw solace from antiquated religious leaders like the Bishops who aren't even able to get their own nuns who actually deal in the real world of health care to follow their lead. They try go back to the Founding Fathers, but the founders of America were a bunch of radicals who were inspired by the French (shudder) Enlightenment philosophers like Voltaire and Rousseau, not to mention English luminaries like John Locke. The Constitution, that precious document they love to cite is essentially a Liberal document. People like Sarah Palin love to reference the Constitution, but her credentials on this subject are woefully inadequate compared to our President who actually taught Constitutional Law at the University of Chicago.

The current outrage in the Congress is that grown men are actually discussing banning birth control for women and there are states controlled by the GOP are actually passing legislation as we speak This sounds like a last gasp of a dinosaur who knows he is doomed but nonetheless grasps for whatever he can bring down with him.

February 16. 2012

Franklin Graham Crosses the Line

I admit never being a big Billy Graham fan. His preaching style was a bit off-putting for me. And his brand of religion was just too restrictive, too prudish for my young sensibilities. But I respected the man. I thought it was great that he struck friendships with all our Presidents, whether they be conservative or liberal, Democrat or Republican. He is a man true to his faith, and has a thorough understanding of the Constitution. He understands the role of religion in our democracy, and he knows that the Constitution that gives him the right to believe what he likes and the freedom to speak his mind also serves to keep politics separate from religion.

In his heyday, he was very careful not to be partisan or political even though he spoke his mind about matters of deep concern to him. And that's the way the Framers of the Constitution intended it to be. Very few people knew of his politics and that was deliberate. Many people assumed, when he was in the spotlight, since he was conservative and an evangelical Christian that he was a Republican. But in fact he was a Democrat but he never let that show. He was strictly non-partisan. He was more interested in the saving of souls rather than meddling in politics

That is not the case with his son Franklin, a product of our current politics of division. Whereas Billy Graham saw himself as a uniter, Franklin has succumbed to the hyper-partisanship of our times. This column will be shorter than usual because we have Franklin Graham in his own words, acting and sounding like a politician on this morning's "Morning Joe." The reader can see for him/herself without the need for great elaboration.

Some people, who have accepted the blurring of the line between politics and religion will see nothing wrong in what Franklin is saying. They will say that he, as a man of faith, is only expressing his views and he is entitled to his views thanks to the first amendment to the Constitution. But there has been a not so subtle shift in our politics. Great religious leaders like Billy Graham and Martin Luther King Jr., to name just two, were passionate about their beliefs and they were very much part of the public square as preachers. They understood their roles and never ventured into partisan politics. Neither Billy Graham nor Dr. King ever criticized the President in public. What they said behind closed doors we do not know, but they were not openly partisan. Yes, Dr. King spoke passionately about injustice and freedom, but he did not equate his passion, which undoubtedly had public policy ramifications, with political partisanship. He wanted every American to fight for his cause, including politicians of all stripes. He did not pick and choose.

Franklin Graham, a product of his time does not see any line between his religious beliefs and his political beliefs. He sounds like a typical politician, not giving straight answers to questions, dodging and weaving and picking sides. And most politically, trying to be on both sides of an issue à la Romney. He is quite deft at it as he probably missed his true calling. He is a pure politician unlike his colleague Rick Warren who is a fellow conservative but stated most eloquently when asked whether he was right or left wing, "I'm for the whole bird." Franklin's answer about whether he thinks the President is a Christian was priceless, for example – yes, he believes him when he claims to be a Christian, but what kind of Christian is he? And according to Muslim Sharia law, President Obama is a Muslim because his dad was a Muslim. Nicely played, reverend.

All of a sudden Sharia law is not only important but a determining factor in America? Still, Reverend Franklin believes the President is a Christian because he went to that Reverend Jeremiah's church but only because he wanted to help folks in Chicago's South Side and that was demanded of him by the community. I lost count. Was that a triple or quadruple bank shot? Politicians out there, take notice. You can learn a lot from this reverend. His slam against Romney was equally dextrous. Romney, like Obama is a good man but not really a Christian, because we all know that Mormons aren't Christians. Bam! And even though he doesn't know what is in Rick Santorum's heart, he knows he is a good Christian. Why? Because he says all the right things (even though he's Catholic). And Newt, the man who has violated most of the ten Commandments is a good man too because he's seen the light (just in time).

Wow.

There is plenty more to say about Franklin Graham of course, but I think it is best to let the man talk for himself. One can only hope that the American public, which is much wiser than the pundits give them credit for will reject this intrusion of religion in our politics. The screamers in Washington have it all wrong as usual. It is not the Government that is intruding in our religious freedoms. It is our religions intruding in our political freedoms. But that is only my opinion. You can judge for yourself.[2]

February 21, 2012

---

2 You can watch the Reverend Graham's appearance on *Morning Joe* on You Tube at: http://www.youtube.com/watch?v=ZP6hU4A3AZY

Santorum Flunks Again

If I was more cynical than I already am, and prone to wild con-spiracy theories I would be tempted to postulate that there is a conspiracy by the remaining GOP candidates to prop up the "in-evitable" candidate Mitt Romney. Others have commented that there is a "gentleman's agreement" between Mitt And Ron Paul since Paul, who is not afraid to criticize anyone, including ex-President Bush, the Republican Party, Wall Street, the Pentagon, and the dreaded liberal media among so many others, so far has not laid a glove on his rival, Romney. Some commentators find this a bit fishy and suggest that Mitt has promised him some-thing we don't know about, say, abolishing the Federal Reserve or getting rid of the Marine Corps or the CIA. Who knows? But I admit it is a bit strange that the outspoken and fearless Paul doesn't utter a peep of disapproval towards the man he needs to beat if he wants to be President.

As far as the other two, both Santorum and Gingrich are doing their level best to say the most mindless things so that Mitt seems almost normal. Gingrich thinks that poor kids should scrub toilets bringing back the 19th century England that led Charles Dickens to write such moving novels as *Oliver Twist* and *David Copperfield* as well as leading German philosopher Karl Marx to write the *Communist Manifesto*. And Santorum, not happy to just be against abortion inveighs against birth control as well, an oxymoronic position if there ever was one. I guess that Rick doesn't care much for women's votes. Perhaps he is for rescinding the right of women to vote as well. I guess he does have a point. Since the gals got the vote and birth control we men can't boss them around as much. Ah, for the good old days when guys ruled the roost.

But Rick was almost there. Mitt, who suffers from severe foot in mouth disease, was begging Santorum to push him off the stage. I mean, making fun of NASCAR folks? That's what the pointy head liberal intellectuals do. But Mitt keeps doing it, over and over again - reminding us that he is vastly superior to the rest of us. Even Republicans, with their pathological fear of the unwashed, do not like to be reminded that rich people think their excrement is not malodorous. In short, in America we sort of consider ourselves to be equal to each other. It probably has something to do with that famous Declaration that Thomas Jefferson wrote so many years ago.

Just when Rick was about to pull a huge upset win in Mitt Romney's home state, thereby possibly derailing Romney's train to the nomination and changing history, he decided it was a swell idea to disrespect the American Dream. Really, Rick? Did you come up with that on your own, or did you get help from your staff, or were you possibly paid off handsomely by the severely prosperous Romney? What are we supposed to think? Either you and/or your staff are colossally soft-witted or you were bought off by the Romney merry band of predators. Either way, Santorum has proved to us (again, see: Santorum Flunks Leadership 101) that neither he nor his posse are ready for the Big Dance.

For those of you who might possibly live on a different planet or do not read the news or own a TV, let me try to explain to Mr. Santorum and his disciples what the American Dream is all about. You see, we live in a country that is **aspirational**. That means that each generation tries to improve its lot in life. Whether you are a conservative, liberal, religious, or non-religious, black, white, recent immigrant or came over on the Mayflower most people want better for their children. They wish for them to succeed. That is their aspiration, hence the term aspirational. So to accuse President Obama, who encourages people to seek post secondary education, of being a snob is so out of character with American values that it cost Santorum the primary election in Michigan and hence the nomination of the Republican Party.

There is plenty of stuff that Republicans disagree with the President on, but the opportunity to send your kids to college is not one of them. Even the most diehard Republican believes in higher education as the best means to success in America. This is not a debate. Nobody is suggesting that we make things more difficult for people to attend college or some sort of training after high school. The President has in both discourse and deed encouraged young people to pursue some type of training or higher education. President Obama is the embodiment of the American Dream, one of the many reasons why Americans voted for him. He doesn't come from wealth and is a racial minority.

But in spite of all the obstacles in his way, the President's mother and then his grandparents helped him achieve one of the pinnacles of success in America: a law degree from Harvard. On the other hand, Santorum just lost the Jewish mother vote with that one.

It is hard to overstate the *faux pas* this was. This is beyond *gaffe, faux pas,* and all the other French words we can bring to this occasion. This shows a lack of a basic understanding of what America is all about. And what makes it cruel on top of callous is that Santorum himself is the holder of three degrees from prestigious universities. So he is in effect saying that what was good for him is not necessarily something to which other people should aspire.

Since I doubt Santorum is this stupid and that he has probably not been bribed by the Romney people to act like a buffoon on purpose, there is something more sinister going on here. And since this attack on Obama was calculated I suspect that he wants to accuse the President of being some sort of dictator. The Republican disinformation machine has already successfully demonized "Obamacare" as they call the *Affordable Heath Care Act* by emphasizing the mandate part without mentioning the benefit parts. The birth control flap raised by the hopelessly out-of-touch Catholic Bishops fell right into his lap, leading him to accuse the President of dictating to the Church what to do. So he thought that he could follow-up on his narrative by obliquely suggesting that Obama's next move was to force kids to go to college whether they need to or want to so they would be formed "in his image," a not so subtle reference to God and intimating that Obama is convinced he is the Almighty himself. There are plenty of frustrated people who have bought into this narrative. And at this point all Santorum cares about is appealing to the ultra Obama haters who think that Romney doesn't hate Obama with the kind of passion they do.

So he has done Gingrich one better. Gingrich just wants poor kids to scrub toilets, but is not adverse to them going to college. Santorum, who unlike Gingrich's obsession with the 19th century, apparently finds comfort in the 17th century where people were told to be satisfied with their lot in life, that it was God's will and they should not aspire to rise above their station. Aside from the obvious cynicism implicit in this kind of retro-rationale, I thought we fought a Revolution against that type of thinking.

February 29, 2012

Rush Must Go!

You will not find a stronger defender of the First Amendment of the Constitution than me. I was one of the very few of my friends who supported the ACLU's decision to support the American Nazi Party marching through a predominantly Jewish neighborhood in Illinois many years ago. People in America, even when they are repulsed by hateful ideology, know that even the most repugnant speech is protected. This is very different than a country such as Germany which has had a very unfortunate history with right-wing extremists and now does not allow Nazis the right of free speech in their own country. Ironically, German Nazis find solace and a safe haven in the United States, the country which helped crush the Nazi movement.

But free speech does have its limitations, even in America. For example, one cannot slander private citizens. Through tradition, there has always been an exception for public figures, even though a few Hollywood actors have sued the more salacious media successfully. But that is rare.

Rush Limbaugh, one of the most obnoxious radio personalities in American history, has been loved by the self-appointed "ditto heads" as his fans are known and reviled by the rest of the country which finds his bombastic, hateful speech deliberately hurtful and offensive. But usually he has been within the confines of the First Amendment and therefore untouchable.

Until now. Rush has finally crossed the line.

He started with calling Georgetown University student Sandra Fluke, who testified before Congress about the importance of woman's access to contraception, a "slut" and a "prostitute." Not content with this initial name-calling, Mr. Limbaugh continued the following day by stating that, *"If we are going to have to pay for this, then we want something in return, Ms. Fluke. And that would be the videos of all this sex posted on line for all of us to see what we are getting for our money."* I have a hard time imagining that any decent person would not find this statement broadcast live to millions of viewers detestable at the least. Our brave Speaker of the House, Republican John Boehner, under pressure from Democrats called the remarks, "inappropriate." Wow, what courage! At the same time, our four Republican Presidential candidates, vying for the job of leader of the free world and commander in chief of the planet's most powerful armed forces have remained thunderously silent. Such profiles in courage for these leadership pretenders.

Rush Limbaugh is just not simply an independent loudmouth on the radio. Limbaugh is the unofficial leader of the Republican Party, the voice that no Republican politician dare speak against. The best the Speaker could muster is the tepid "inappropriate" and even that tepid statement will bring down the wrath of the monster that is Rush. Don't be surprised if the intrepid Speaker revises his remarks to say that he meant to say that "some people" find Limbaugh's remarks inappropriate. This is the party that routinely calls the President of the United States every name in the book, but it cowers to the bully that is Rush Limbaugh. One has to wonder, if Rush is so powerful and important to the GOP why they just don't run him for President.

There are things that can be done about this travesty of a man within the law, however. Pushing the reprehensible aside, Rush actually committed an illegal act. It is illegal to slander a private individual. The civil courts can remedy this situation. It is hard to believe that there hasn't been a major law firm stepping up to represent Sandra Fluke in an action against Limbaugh and his employers pro bono. I can't think of an easier slam dunk. I would hope there are conversations within major law firms as we speak.

And what of the commercial sponsors of the man with the golden microphone? Is the fact that he commands millions of listeners important enough to sponsors as to ignore such an offensive bully for a little market share? In the vulgar parlance of Rush himself, who are the real prostitutes here? Women's organizations should organize a campaign to target the show's sponsors. He is a paper tiger living on bluster and needs to get more and more outrageous in order to keep up the interest of his audience. Glenn Beck ran out of drivel and was tossed off Fox News because he was getting more and more over the top even for them.

Rush Limbaugh has a guaranteed right to say what he likes under our Constitution. What the Constitution does not protect him from is slandering an ordinary citizen and, more to the point, there is no guarantee that he should be paid to expectorate on the public airwaves. Getting paid to speak your mind is a privilege not a right.

There are some on the left who enjoy Rush Limbaugh's tirades because he makes liberals look good. Rush is one of the best advertisements for the Democrats. If Barack Obama wins re-election he will have Rush to thank in part because he has reduced the GOP to a caricature of what it used to be. The spectacle of Republican politicians genuflecting to this misanthrope is too precious for liberals to pass up. But at what cost to the Republic? It may be great fun to play tit-for-tat with snake-oil merchants like Rush - it makes his fans squeal with joy when he serves up red meat night after night, and his detractors delighted to point out the fatuousness of his opinions. Professional politicos make tons of money egging their supporters to counter his rants. Thus, both the left and right are invested in this varmint and the toxicity of our public discourse just grows and grows. America just cannot afford the sideshow that is Rush Limbaugh anymore. Maybe it was fun while it lasted but our country has serious business to take care of now. It is time for Rush to go.

Post Script: It has come to my attention that Rush Limbaugh gets taxpayer money to broadcast his show on Armed Services Radio. This is an outrage that this man who is so disrespectful towards the commander in chief be paid to pollute the minds of our servicemen. There is an opportunity for people to sign petitions to remove Limbaugh from AFN and stop receiving our tax dollars.

Update: The list of sponsors of the Rush Limbaugh show is diminishing as we speak. By last count it is up to 90 as of this date: 3/12/2012. But that is not the good news. The good news is that sponsors are revising their commitment to what is increasingly known as hate speech as opposed to polemical speech. Having strong opinions is the life blood of a democracy and no one should be deprived of their constitutional rights of free speech no matter how vehemently you disagree with them. But there is a small group of popular talk show hosts who routinely cater to racism, sexism, and bigotry who should not have a place in our society, propped up by either tax dollars or private sector sponsors who ultimately need to appeal to consumers who have choices as to where they spend their money. I chose to write a blog that is free from interference. I don't get paid millions of dollars and therefore am not accountable to anyone except my readers and my conscious. Rush can do the same and he lives in a country where there is no censorship by the government. However when people spew hate for profit, one has to consider the consequences for the folks who pay for this hate. Sponsors, thanks to Limbaugh's over the top behavior are re-examining their commitment to make money off of people's insecurities and prejudices. We all owe a debt of gratitude to Rush for making these issues painfully obvious so that sponsors are now going to be much more careful where they use their advertising dollars. I hope they are sophisticated enough to know the difference between hate for money and controversy. Controversy is a good thing regardless of where it comes from, hate is always bad. Controversy makes you think. Hate shuts down the mind. We will be a better country if our discussions are hot but without deliberate personal invective. If that happens we will have Rush to thank.

March 3, 2012

Religion and Civilization

There was a time when Islamic culture had a great civilizing influence on the planet. Islamic scholars, for example, preserved many of the significant texts of Western Civilization. When monks in the Middle Ages were painstakingly making beautiful hand made copies of the Bible, complete with exquisite calligraphy and gorgeous illustrations, Muslim scholars were busy preserving the works of Aristotle and Plato, the founding fathers of democracy.

In modern times there are people living today who remember the days when large parts of the Middle East were cosmopolitan. Beirut was commonly known as the "Paris" of the Middle East, a modern multicultural city with beauteous boulevards lined with sidewalk cafés. Countries like Tunisia and Morocco were favorite tourist destinations as were countries like Egypt and Syria. Islam, by and large was a "big tent" religion and very tolerant of other religions, especially with what the Koran calls "people of the book." People of the book refers to Christians and Jews and the Koran makes it explicit that Christians and Jews are related by tradition to Islam. Americans either don't know or seem to forget that Jesus himself is considered a Muslim prophet. And looking back in time the Koran speaks eloquently of Judeo-Christian shared prophets such as Abraham. The Koran goes to great lengths to show the common heritage of Islam with Judaism and Christianity.

So what happened? In a word: fundamentalism.

The word fundamentalism has taken a very misfortunate meaning. Not only – but principally – with respect to religion. If one looks up fundamentalism in Webster, the very first definition is a reference to the American Protestant movement of the 20th century. The older and more "fundamental" meaning, which is a strict adherence to a basic set of principles has been given not only second status, but is still connected to religion, as in "fundamentalist Islam."

Why is this important, and not simply an exercise in etymology?

There is nothing intrinsically wrong with the concept of fundamentalism. Having a strong set of principles is generally a good thing. Having strong basic beliefs is important when living in an ever changing world. However, taking a text verbatim that was written several thousand years ago is dubious at best. Take the Ten Commandments, the "basis" of Judeo-Christian law. Remember the judge who had a plaque hanging in his courthouse? Want to stump a Christian or a Jew? Ask them to name all ten commandments. The answers will be stunning. There are some of the commandments that are great. **Do not kill**, for example. But how many Jews and Christians really believe that? Keep the Sabbath holy? Jews and Christians can't even agree on which day the "Sabbath" falls, much less as to what is acceptable or not to do on that day.

So relying on a literal reading of an ancient text is problematic at best. What seems more important to me, is to glean from a reading of scripture what values are right for you in your particular time.

Islamic fundamentalists have cherry-picked parts of the Koran which reinforce their retrograde and paranoid view of the world and have turned their views into a nightmare for the world, but most specifically for the Muslim world itself. Beirut is a shadow of what it was, and the entire Middle East is mired in petty wars which pit brother against brother in an endless and futile pursuit of power. The ordinary Muslim citizen is paying the price. What used to be the cradle of civilization has been turned into a cesspool. All of this in a quest for religious purity. Using a holy book, not to spread peace and love, but to spread hate and violence.

Christian and Jewish fundamentalists are the first ones to point out the folly of Muslim fundamentalism. There have been Koran burnings as one extreme response to the threat of fundamentalist Islam but more typically there have been efforts to ban Mosques and to badmouth Muslims in general. Remember, for a sizable percentage of Republican voters, President Obama is a Muslim and therefore "unqualified" to be President even though the Constitution clearly states there is no religious qualification to be President. So much for fundamentalist readings of the Constitution, but that will be for another conversation. Forget about the pesky fact that the President is a Christian.

It is not a big stretch to say that if fundamentalist Islam has contributed to the downgrading of Muslim civilization, then what is the role of fundamentalist Christianity regarding our own civilization? Watching the rise of this type of Christianity in our political discourse one cannot help but observe the paranoia, the retro thinking, and like the fundamentalist Islamists, the focus of their wrath is mostly towards women. We bemoan the treatment of the Taliban towards women yet there are signs that American fundamentalist infused politicians in America are promoting ideas such as trying to force women to subject themselves to vaginal probes. Under non-state conditions, forcing a woman to endure a vaginal probe against her will is simply called rape. Still there are some legislators who will rail against government intrusion but apparently think that jamming a probe in a woman's vagina against her will is peachy keen.

Unfortunately, the above mentioned assault is but the tip of the iceberg. Humiliating a college student because she had the temerity to agree with the President that contraception should be covered by medical insurance goes far beyond the vile language exhibited by Rush Limbaugh which is why his apology for his use of language is so hollow. The "war against women" is not simply a Democratic Party slogan. (although it also is that as well) It is very real. The fundamentalists in our country are totally paranoid about the growing influence and power of women. Nothing frightens the patriarchy more than emancipated women running amok and free just like men. This is mostly a "white" male phenomenon with the complicity of their suckered, bullied and/or battered female companions. They feel like they are losing their grip on power so they lash out against – and for a lack of a better word – *modernity*.

"Taking our country back," is the last desperate cry of the paranoid fringe who pine for a simpler time when everybody knew their place. Read: women knew their place. So the fringe lashes out. They lash out against the black guy in the White House to whom they refer as the "usurper." They lash out against Hispanics who they think promote illegal "aliens." And they lash out against Muslims who they think are all some sort of terrorist sympathizers, terrorists or terrorists in waiting. It is all so pathetic and such a waste of time and effort.

If we look at the effect of the Muslim fundamentalists on their own culture it is a sobering thought to think something similar could be happening in our country, the most liberal of all liberal democracies in the world. A country that in spite of all its flaws and mistakes is still held forth as the best hope for humanity. Fortunately, there are many counter-currents in America today. Rick Santorums's ascendency will be regarded as a small blip in the wide span of American History, and in spite of all the gains of the fundamentalists in our country, their efforts will ultimately be futile. And judging by the youth of America, there is hope. Although there is plenty of hand wringing about young people today (and I hand-wring as well as the next person) I have every confidence the youth of today will blossom into an enlightened generation and will carry on America as the bastion of innovation and progress it has always been.

March 15, 2012

Exploiting Fear for Profit

We have grown accustomed as a country to those who exploit fear and bigotry for profit. The two names that come easily to mind are Rush Limbaugh and Glenn Beck, two of the more successful practitioners of this sinister science. While conservatives are all in a knot over the perceived injustice of picking on Rush because he disrespects women (I thought only whiny leftists worried about injustice) the bigger picture is missed. Rush, Glenn, and all the other stars of the "vast right-wing conspiracy" are not really reviled due to their use of language (what Rush thought he did wrong) or their persistent picking on the President (which is why they think liberals hate them). No, their "sin" is not because they constantly lie about the President and his policies, their main offense is that they peddle fear for profit.

We live in uncertain times and there are changes afoot. (Remember, we voted for change.) But many people, especially older folks like myself, are very leery of change. Skeptical of all this newfangled world we don't understand very well. Too much technology that scares us. Things move too fast. The world is in turmoil. Not like the good old days where everything was familiar. The Russians had the bomb and were Communist. That was simple to understand. They were bad, we were good. To make that point clearer, we added the word "God" to our pledge of allegiance to make sure we were clear that God was not on the side of the Communists. Congress added the words "under God" to the pledge in 1954 at the peak of the Cold War. After all, the pledge had been written by Francis Bellamy a Socialist, and who wanted a Socialist pledge? Especially when fighting the Commies.

Anyway, those were familiar times. Hiding under your school desk in case of a nuclear attack seemed like a rational response. Those were the good old days when nobody said "shit" on TV and women kept their bras on.

But now, everything's different. People say shit (and worse) on TV. There are a lot of bra-less women on the screen. And there's a black family in the White House. Wow, that is just too much to absorb for old farts like me. So enter the purveyors of fear. Now mind you, they didn't invent fear. They just exploit it. For *beaucoup* bucks. I mean really a lot of jack, Mac. It seems if you are shameless and play on people's phobias you get remunerated to the umpteenth degree.

But there's a new wrinkle I was not aware of. And it is more pervasive than I thought and under- reported by the so-called lame-stream media. Now that a significant segment of the population is afraid of the future, the new hottest cottage in-dustry is investment "counseling" based on fear. Yes, Virginia, there are many more ways we can fleece the perennially paranoid. The following is a word for word statement by one of these "advisers:"

"I can honestly say I've never been more afraid for the future of America than I am right now.

"YOU MAY NOT LIKE WHAT I'M ABOUT TO REVEAL. IT'S CERTAINLY NOT FOR THE FAINT OF HEART. YOU MAY NOT EVEN BELIEVE IT. BUT I ASSURE YOU IT IS TRUE!

"I've created an urgent presentation to warn you about what I expect to be the single most menacing economic crisis of your lifetime. "Ignore this warning and you may as well take your savings... your retirement... and your financial security and kiss them goodbye."

You are then led to a lengthy video that keeps up the fear mongering and dire predictions of impending doom and ends with a pitch for a subscription to a newsletter. Now there is nothing particularly new or innovative here. What is new is how the right-wing fear machine is branching out into the personal financial advice business. If Rush, Glenn, et. al., can soak sponsors why not use the same fear techniques to chisel chumps?

Here's where it gets weird. Since conservatives don't believe in regulation and pray to the almighty god of the free marketplace, they think it is OK for predators to pluck their own. Liberals, who are generally unaffected by these scams are OK with them as long as the victims are right-wingers. So everybody's happy, right?

Well, not exactly. I suppose that for liberals it is comforting to think of the victims as Neanderthal beer swilling "ditto-heads" who richly deserve getting hoisted on their own petard I, however think of the victims as more likely to be scared old ladies who lost their husbands and who were hopelessly wedded to the likes of a Sean Hannity but now have nowhere to turn so they might trust a scam artist with their life savings who have similar views to those of their deceased husbands.

At any rate, nobody deserves to be scammed. It is disgusting that conservatives prey on their own but these charlatans should be denounced by anyone with a conscience as the shameful predators that they are. Is it too much to hope for that they will be hauled off to prison? Just sayin'...

March 19, 2012

Religion and Civilization Part II

*The following article is written in a form of an open letter to Andrew Sullivan a man I much admire for his wit and candor and for his erudition. I don't expect to match Mr. Sullivan's erudition but am prepared to rebut his well written and thoughtful piece, "Christianity in Crisis," an article that I am in essentially agreement with, especially with respect to Sullivan's critique of modern Christianity. He claims that Christianity has become too intertwined with partisan politics. His arguments are provocative and persuasive. He starts with Thomas Jefferson, always a winner in my view, who's incredible **chutzpah**, to borrow an expression from the Jews, led him to editing the Holy Book. And not just any holy book, the Christian Bible.*

Dear Andrew (may I call you Andrew?),

I think it took immense courage for you to take on the religious zealots of our time. One of my favorite historical figures, Galileo, was excommunicated for his discovery that the Earth was not the center of the universe. Imagine how that must have shaken the fibers of the Church which was so invested in the idea that we were put on this earth by a divine being who controls everything. And to find out the divine being they prayed to, the immutable spirit, that all encompassing deity, did not even bother to make us the center of the universe! No wonder Galileo was reviled in his day and it took centuries for the Church to come around and apologize for its horrendous behavior towards him. In fact, it was finally only in 1992 when the Vatican officially apologized to Galileo. The Church of England, ever so much quicker on the draw, apologized to Darwin in 2008, a mere 126 years after his death. I guess we should call it progress. But to this day, although there are very few people who doubt Galileo, there are still many (mostly in America, I'm afraid) who still have their doubts about Darwin.

So Jefferson tried to save Jesus from the Christians. And yes, he painstakingly used a razor to extract what he thought were the essential teachings of that great man. The *Jefferson Bible* people call it these days, but I seriously doubt Jefferson would have liked that. Actually the title he gave the book which was not intended for public consumption was *The Life and Morals of Jesus of Nazareth Extracted Textually from the Gospels* which kind of tells you something about Jefferson right there. There is very little hint of the divine in that title. You might even say there is an attempt by Jefferson to extract the teachings of the man from a religious book. His quaint expression, as you quote him, Andrew, is "taking the diamonds from the dunghill." Not exactly how I would have phrased it but then Jefferson was quite the man of letters.

This is where I (and Jefferson himself) part company with you, Andrew. You cleverly omitted a key word from Jefferson's vocabulary in your piece. A word that defines what Jefferson fought against, as well as many of our Founding Fathers. That word is *superstition*. Let that sink in a bit, Andrew.

Superstition.

Cannot say it enough. Because if there was one thing Jefferson disliked above all other things, it was superstition. Here's a taste:

"I have examined all the known superstitions of the world, and I do not find in our particular superstition of Christianity one redeeming feature. They are all alike founded on fables and mythology. Millions of innocent men, women and children, since the introduction of Christianity, have been burnt, tortured, fined and imprisoned. What has been the effect of this coercion? To make one half the world fools and the other half hypocrites; to support roguery and error all over the earth."

You have to dig deep (but not that deep) to get to Jefferson's feelings about religion and about Christianity in particular. Jefferson admired the person he called Jesus of Nazareth. He thought his teachings were among the best in the world and Jefferson was an accomplished scholar so he had access to all the biggies. Jefferson thought it would be illuminating to have a compilation of the teachings of Jesus without the accompanying "superstitions" which are all references to miracles and the other stuff that makes his teaching a religion, not a philosophy. There are plenty of Marxists out there who believe in the teachings of Marx without the benefit of divine intervention. Only the deeply delusional would call that "religion." The essence of Jefferson's message: Jesus had a lot to teach us but all the religious trappings that go with these teachings are not necessary for us to respect and follow the man. When he said he was a Christian he meant it in the same way that people who follow Marx call themselves Marxists.

Andrew, I do not begrudge your religion. You are among my favorites. Your stands against the Church's bigotry toward gays are colossal in their bravery. People have been hanged for less. That you take on the **religious/political complex** is admirable beyond belief. Religion has poisoned politics not only here but everywhere. At least here we can safely say that Christians in their zeal don't do anything more harmful than support a dweeb like Santorum or pass laws forcing women to undergo vaginal probes for no medical reason. We can be thankful that ritual stoning of women is not promoted here. Or that we don't condone female genital mutilation like they do in so many other countries. So far the fanatics in our country have seen fit to simply insert "Creationism" as a valid scientific theory or try to make abortions illegal like the good old days when desperate women were butchered by unscrupulous "providers". Yes we have to be thankful for all that, and I thank you from the bottom of my heart that you are trying to make religious people as reasonable as possible.

But (here comes the "but") please do not use my guy Jefferson to make your point. I am an unapologetic disciple of the En-lightenment philosophers like Voltaire, Rousseau, and John Locke, as was Jefferson, and it is our contention that superstition, dressed up as religion is the bane of this world. You want to believe in talking snakes, magical underwear, or 72 virgins that is your affair. But Jefferson is not the guy to use to buttress your faith in the supernatural. That he didn't believe in the supernatural, is obvious if you read his letters. Religious people point to his famous phrase in the Declaration:

"We hold these truths to be self-evident, that all men are created equal, that they are endowed by their Creator with certain unalienable Rights, that among these are Life, Liberty and the pursuit of Happiness."

to mean that Jefferson was a Christian in the sense we understand Christianity. Jefferson, like Benjamin Franklin and Thomas Paine, was a Deist. Deists believe in what they call a Natural God, a God bereft of all "revealed" religions. Revealed religions are so named because they all make claim to having received a special revelation from God. All of the World's major religions are "revealed religions". The revelations range from the acceptance of the ten commandments by Moses to the rather self serving discovery by Joseph Smith of the "golden plates" where it was revealed that Jesus himself visited the United States.

Deism, on the other hand is a belief that there is a higher principle we can call God that is responsible for our world and its intricacies. It is not a "he" nor can it be talked to or even petitioned. God is simply a way to talk about the natural order of things, or nature if you will. This was Jefferson's core belief and it is clear in not only the Declaration but in his writings as well. Jefferson did not believe it was necessary to invent a supernatural rather that everything was by definition "natural". It was man's role to try to discover the mysteries of the natural world, not to invent superstitions to try to explain what we cannot fathom. That is why he wanted a "wall of separation" between the State and religion to make sure the two did not impede on each other. He was a realist so he did not try to ban religion, just to keep it separate from public policy.

This is Jefferson's gift to all of us. Use him to justify democracy, liberty, natural law, but not to justify religion. Andrew, you're going to have to find someone else for that.

Yours truly,

Peter Calvet

April 2, 2012

"Stand Your Ground"

776.013   Home protection; use of deadly force; presumption of fear of death or great bodily harm. *A person is presumed to have held a reasonable fear of imminent peril of death or great bodily harm to himself or herself or another when using defensive force that is intended or likely to cause death or great bodily harm to another if: (a)   The person against whom the defensive force was used was in the process of unlawfully and forcefully entering, or had unlawfully and forcibly entered, a dwelling, residence, or occupied vehicle, or if that person had removed or was attempting to remove another against that person's will from the dwelling, residence, or occupied vehicle; and (b)   The person who uses defensive force knew or had reason to believe that an unlawful and forcible entry or unlawful and forcible act was occurring or had occurred.*

There is a lot of confusion about Florida's controversial "Stand Your Ground" law. Not content with the anachronistic Second Amendment to the Constitution which is spelled out in my article in <u>Salon,</u> the NRA (America's armaments business lobby) was the inspiration of a law in Florida and several other states that takes the pretty much universal rule of self-defense and embellishes it – as if self defense weren't clear enough. In this case, the law is appealing to the home owner for special protection. It is not enough, apparently to know that if a thug with murderous intentions approaches you in the woods, or the mall or wherever, you have an intrinsic right of self protection. Any schoolkid knows that and it is quite straightforward enough. If someone is about to kill you, you have the right to kill him first. Doesn't take a law degree from Harvard to comprehend the obvious.

But it takes the slick lawyers at the NRA to turn something simple into into a set political piece. Not content with the simplicity of self-defense, the NRA went about doing what they ordinarily would complain about the government doing, which is to complicate the issue with a lot of double talk and legalese when none was required. One should recall the American popular folklore phrase, "If it ain't broke, don't fix it." By and large Americans, to a fault, believe that is precisely what is basically wrong with government. It is not a mystery that the crusade against health care reform found resonance in part because most Americans didn't think that their health care was broken and therefore the Obama cure was worse than the disease. Unfortunately, they were wrong, but they usually only find out how bad it is when it affects them directly – like when their sister couldn't get her operation paid for because the insurance company found a preexisting condition. By then it is too late. It is possible for things to get fixed if they are indeed broken, but you have to know they are broken first. I digress.

In the case of self-defense law, there was nothing broken, The NRA was just making a political ploy towards those most politically vulnerable members of society, the suburban homeowner, er, swing voter. By singling out the homeowners, the NRA was saying to them that "we care about you." They know suburban homeowners are particularly insecure, especially the ones with children. There is no one more easily scared than a family with small children. So the "Stand your Ground" law reads like a manual for the homeowner. *"The person against whom the defensive force was used was in the process of unlawfully and forcefully entering, or had unlawfully and forcibly entered, a dwelling, residence...*

It cries out that you should be protected in your own home and you shouldn't have to worry about the consequence of killing another person if someone is attempting to break into your residence. You see, under the conventional self-defense law, it was necessary to have an actual bodily threat to invoke self defense. Your life had to be in jeopardy in order to justify killing another human being. Under the "Stand your Ground" law, no such imminent lethal threat is necessary. Just the act of breaking into your home is sufficient. Whether it is a kid with a bad case of the munchies, or a burglar after your TV, or a mass murderer makes no difference. You are the king of your castle and if anybody breaks into your domain uninvited you now have the right to execute him under this brilliant piece of legislation brought to you from the good folks of the NRA.

There will be some defenders of the law who will say that people will misinterpret the law, and that will be undoubtedly be the case in the Zimmerman saga. The Martin kid was clearly not trying to break in the house, so the law doesn't even apply, or does it? *"The person who uses defensive force know or had reason to believe that an unlawful and forcible entry or unlawful and forcible act was occurring or had occurred."*

Reason to believe? Now there is a loophole worthy of a politician about to defraud the taxpayer. If I say I had "reason to believe" then that's OK? And what would allow me to have reason to believe? That the kid was wearing a hoodie as the wise Geraldo Rivera might say? Or perhaps he was just a kid. (You know what they are capable of.) Or, of course, a minority – perhaps even an illegal alien. What a great opportunity to bag an Illegal. "I swear he looked like he might be entering the house illegally." Makes sense – he's already here illegally. So the good folks at the NRA not only brought us a law that justifies homicide based on the flimsiest of evidence, but set the stage for slowly recreating the good old days of the Wild West all in a cynical ploy to garner more votes for the pro-gun crowd and create more clients for their deadly products. Bravo, you should all be proud of yourselves.

April 12, 2012

The Good Wife

One has to admit that Mitt Romney married well. Ann Lois Davies was born into privilege as was her husband. Her father, Edward R. Davies is a classic American self-made man. Originally from Wales, Great Britain he became president of Jered Industries, a maker of heavy machinery for marine use. He dabbled in politics as he was once mayor of Bloomfield Hills, Michigan, a tiny ultra-wealthy town of almost 4,000 whose medium income is a staggering $200,000. In 2009 half of residential property in Bloomfield Hills had a value of over $1,000,000 which is incredibly high for a Midwest small town. Bloomfield Hills consistently ranks as one of the top five wealthiest municipalities in the United States with population between 2,500 to 9,999.

Ann attended the private Kingswood School, the sister school of the private all-boys Cranbrook School that Mitt Romney attended. Their romance began at an early age and was the stuff of story books.

Whereas Mitt can come across as stiff and unsympathetic, Ann comes across as genuine and sympathetic. She has an easy-going demeanor about her which is why when Hilary Rosen attacked her famously for not having "worked a day in her life" people instinctively came to her defense. Also, she has had her share of challenges, contracting multiple sclerosis in 1998 and also endured a brief bout with a fairly benign form of breast cancer in 2008. Fortunately, Ann underwent successful treatment and has since lived a generally disease free life. After her bout with multiple sclerosis, she became an equestrian, excelling at horse dressage where she won a number of prizes. She credits her involvement with horses as having "saved her life" giving her the uplift she needed after her ordeal.

Ann became a stay at home wife and raised five boys and lived the life of relative privilege combining her equestrian activities and her charity work with mom duties such as a member of the PTA . She was also active in the League of Women Voters and taught some cooking classes. None of these activities were particularly unusual for a woman of her social standing, making the Hilary Rosen critique sound unnecessarily strident.

But if you examine Rosen's comments in context, she was talking about how Mitt Romney was not connecting well with women. Romney has said that he talks to his wife about what woman are saying, as if he needs a special ambassador to inform him about the arcane land of women. Apparently his ambassador, who happens to be his wife, is telling him women care about the economy as much as men do. The conversation on CNN hosted by Anderson Cooper was about how women's jobs were not coming back as fast as men's jobs. Rosen simply stated that Ann was not the best person to represent working women because she "never worked a day in her life." Admittedly, that was an awkward way to put it, but since the statement was directed at adults, it was assumed that she was talking about women working outside the home at a paying job. If Republicans didn't routinely decry the culture of "Political Correctness" they could have been forgiven for making such a mountain out of a statement that was obviously political shorthand.

One can fault Rosen, a professional, for not being sufficiently on her toes to recognize her insensitive remark was going to be used as political football during the silly season. However, there is a more sinister side to the Rosen flap. Pundits were quick to point out that Romney needs to repair whatever damage has been done by his party with women voters, but forcing Rosen to apologize to stay-at-home-moms everywhere really misses the point Rosen was making. First, she clearly was not talking about all stay-at-home-moms. She was talking about Ann Romney, a woman of privilege who has many more choices in life than the average woman. Not every woman is married to a multimillionaire, and when Anne had previously said, "I don't even consider myself wealthy..." that didn't fire up the outrage machine for very long.

It is absolutely true that being a mom is hard work. Whether you are a stay at home mom or a "working mom" it is not a cakewalk. We all know that. But women's issues, although many based on being mothers, are not just confined to motherhood. The Republican Party has recently been guilty of many assaults on women, mostly poor women. So for a rich woman who doesn't want people to think of her as rich to be a spokesperson for women, especially poor women, is only going to work if she acknowledges what average women go through on a daily basis and addresses their issues directly, not hiding behind "Motherhood." That she didn't even begin to do.

Ann Romney is a far better spokesperson than her husband. But she cannot rely on politically incorrect statements from the likes of Hilary Rosen to make her husband seem more palatable to women. There are real issues to talk about and it is high time that both Romneys learn what they are. They need to offer new solutions than the ones being proposed by their party or else they will lose the female vote even more dramatically than Republicans usually do.

April 25, 2012

The Paul Ryan Paradox

Many people say that radio commentator Rush Limbaugh is the *de facto* leader of the Republican Party. Nothing could be so absurd. The college dropout Limbaugh – his own mother went so far as saying, "he flunked everything" – is at best a cheerleader for the Republicans, but not in the conventional sense of the word. After all, cheerleaders are a cheery lot, full of positive thoughts and attempt to encourage their team to excel with shouts like, "go team, go!" Rush is the kind of cheerleader that would stand on the sidelines and egg the crowd to chant, "You suck! You suck!" Rush is one in a long line of frustrated individuals if it were not for radio and millions of other frustrated individuals out there he would be a stock boy at his local Wal-Mart. There is very little leadership in him. He has no genuine ideas, offers no solutions and the thought of his being an inspiration for a great traditional political party is just nuts.

Not so for Paul Ryan. Ryan is a graduate from Miami University in Oxford, Ohio, with a BA in economics and political science in 1992. And as a good Republican he made his money the old-fashioned way, he inherited it. Well, maybe inheriting is too strong a word – he got a job as a marketing consultant with Ryan Incorporated Central, which is run by a branch of his family. Not exactly the silver spoon treatment *à la* Bush and Romney, but he did not have to exert a huge effort either, which partly explains his disdain for underprivileged people. I mean, everybody should have the opportunity to work for the family business. Life would be so less complicated that way.

Ryan is a much better candidate than Rush to be the *de facto* leader of the Republicans. At least Ryan has ideas, bold ideas. And he is not shy about committing them to paper. He shows leadership by getting his colleagues, even presumptive nominee for President Mitt Romney to follow his lead. That is the stuff of leadership. Present bold ideas and not limit yourself to the sidelines with perennial posturing.

Here is where it starts getting a bit weird, though. Ryan's budget, the blueprint for Republican public policy has been endorsed by all the bigwigs in the Party, including the "anything goes" Mitt Romney. Ryan tells us that his Catholic faith was his inspiration.

Not quite from Jesus Himself but almost. He wants us to feel the Christian compassion in his choices for America. But the Catholic Bishops – remember the guys who accused President Obama of being anti-religious – those Catholic Bishops? They said that Ryan's budget wasn't so Christian after all. As a matter of fact, they said, "A just spending bill cannot rely on disproportionate cuts in essential services to poor and vulnerable persons." The good Bishops even said that his budget "fails to meet" the moral criteria of the Church. That is some strong stuff coming from the group that not too long ago complained that the President was forcing them to provide contraception to non-Catholic workers at Catholic institutions.

This time the Bishops sound really steamed. It is one thing to foist contraception on women who want it and need it, it is quite another to complain that Ryan's bill is immoral. Not to pile on but a group of Jesuit scholars at Georgetown University went so far as to say, "[the budget] appears to reflect the values of your favorite philosopher, Ayn Rand, rather than the Gospel of Jesus Christ. Her call to selfishness and her antagonism toward religion are antithetical to the Gospel values of compassion and love."

Ouch.

And the good Jesuits have a point. In 2005 Ryan admitted, "The reason I got involved in public service, by and large, if I had to credit one thinker, one person, it would be Ayn Rand." Not to be content with his personal preferences, New York magazine has claimed that Ryan "requires staffers to read *Atlas Shrugged*." *Atlas Shrugged* is probably Ayn Rand's best novel and it is a scathing attack on Christian values that she claims are antithetical to Capitalism. The Church leaders and Rand seem to agree on this point. That Ayn Rand's atheistic philosophy regards the Christian message as a major impediment to a true Capitalist based economy. And it seems like the young Ryan, himself a beneficiary of the Capitalist system was keen on jettisoning his Catholic faith for the more prosperity oriented Ayn Rand who is happy to assert (since she didn't have to run for anything) that the markets are a better moral compass than the teachings of Jesus. No wonder Mitt Romney is on board. This is right up his alley. I can almost picture a young 10 year old Romney convincing a school mate that he would be better off if he took his bike apart and sold the parts. Of course, the youngster Mitt would take a sizable chunk of the profit because, after all, it was his idea. But I digress...

The *de facto* leader of the Republicans (watch your back, John Boehner!) is not undaunted. He claims that although his budget might be more in tune with Rand than with Jesus, he is definitely not a subscriber to Rand's philosophy. The fact that he got interested in public service due to Rand's teachings and not the gospels is irrelevant. Also irrelevant is that he goes so far as suggesting to his staff that they read Ayn Rand. He went even further and said quite recently, "It's a big stretch to suggest that a person is therefore an Objectivist... I reject her philosophy. It's an atheist philosophy. It reduces human interactions down to mere contracts and it is antithetical to my worldview. If somebody is going to try to paste a person's view on epistemology to me, then give me Thomas Aquinas. Don't give me Ayn Rand."

I think the Bishops would be quite pleased if Ryan had based his budget on Aquinas. The Catholic Saint famously said that things that pertain to all men are reduced to seven headings: Faith, Hope, and Charity; Prudence, Justice, Fortitude, and Temperance. If only Ryan's budget were based on these principles I think the Bishops would have few problems with him. But unfortunately for Ryan, these precepts are hardly present in his budget which gives to the rich and takes away from the poor. Not exactly what Jesus would do. The saintly Aquinas would be disappointed.

Whatever happened to Compassionate Conservatism? It almost makes one yearn for George W.

May 2, 2012

The Real Job Creators

"It's the economy, stupid." Those prophetic words uttered by James Carville characterized the rise of Bill Clinton and were the driving force behind his upset win over George Bush senior, considered by many a shoo-in for a second term.

Mitt Romney, hardly a fan when Clinton was President, currently praises the Clinton economy and has staked his run for the Presidency on making the case that he has what it takes to turn this economy around. He claims that Barack Obama is hopelessly in over his head. Romney boasts he is a "job creator" a phrase that no doubt has come from the laboratory of the dark Dr. Frank Luntz (see, "The Most Dangerous Man in America" on this blog). But whatever its origin, this phrase has become the mantra for the entire Republican Party with little push back from the Democrats who usually don't know when they are being played.

Romney posits his company Bain Capital as Exhibit A. Exhibit B is his successfully turnaround of the Winter Olympics. Exhibit C is his stint as Governor which he will only talk about if severely water-boarded.

The reasons Romney is loathe to speak of Exhibit C are obvious. First, he was the one who came up with "Romneycare," the father of "Obamacare," that he claims is an abomination and which he will repeal the first day he gets into office. Let us put aside the impossibility of eliminating "Obamacare" with a stroke of a pen because it would be violating the Constitution, a minor point to be sure, but as a newly elected President he would be wise to conform to the law for at least a day or so. Romney's problem is that his party has demonized "Obamacare" so much that he cannot take credit for his only real achievement as Governor of Massachusetts.

It gets worse. His claim to be a "job creator" flies in the face of his miserable performance as the Governor of the Bay State when it was ranked 47th out of 50 states on this topic. Very hard to explain that considering Massachusetts has some of the best universities in the world and is a high tech center with innovations only rivaled by Silicon Valley in California. His claim to fame as a great job creator while leading a state leaves something to be desired so he has decided wisely to keep quiet about it hoping nobody will notice.

Exhibit B is just as problematic as Exhibit C but for different reasons. Yes, Romney was the hero of the Salt Lake City Olympics. He inherited a scandal and ended in a profit. There is no question that without Mitt Romney the Salt Lake games would have been a bust. He did indeed put shoulder to the wheel – he bowed and scraped, saved here and there and raised funds from private sector companies that had never pitched in before. He lived and breathed Olympics. But there is one small detail that gets lost in all the laudatory praise heaped on Romney's white knight role. He successfully lobbied the Federal government for a cool $1.5 billion. Yes, the games generated a $100 million dollar profit which he likes to brag about, but without the $1.5 billion from the Feds he would still be paying off debts. Thus, Mitt has to tread lightly on the turnaround of the Olympics as a feat of his private sector job creating prowess. Maybe, due to the events of 9/11, the country needed a shot in the arm and the $1.5 billion was money well spent, even though many leaders of his own party were against this kind of bailout. Ultimately, however, the taxpayer was the final decider of success in that particular venture, not Romney.

Exhibit A is Mitt's strongest suit. Some might even say, his only suit. And this is where Bain Capital comes in. Here's a taste of how they see themselves:

> *"Established in 1984, Bain Capital is one of the world's leading private investment firms managing approximately $60 billion in assets under management. Our affiliated advisers make private equity, public equity, leveraged debt asset, venture capital, and absolute return investments across multiple sectors, industries, and asset classes. Since our inception, our competitive advantage has been grounded in a people-intensive, value-added investment approach that has enabled the firm to deliver industry-leading returns for our investors."*

Nowhere in this description is there even a hint at job creation. Not even company creation. The emphasis is on the delivery of "industry-leading returns for our investors." That is the bottom line for Bain and for Romney himself. And their track record speaks for itself: What ever it takes to make a buck. Sometimes companies thrived and Romney is quick to point out his successes which are not trivial. Companies like Steel Dynamics, Staples and Sports Authority were indeed rescued by Bain. In these cases there was more money to be made keeping the companies alive. But that was almost incidental, because in other cases, piling on debt and liquidating was the better way to turn a profit. Companies, for Romney and the folks at Bain, are just instruments to generate profits for themselves. It matters little if the company thrives, goes under, or is shipped overseas. Romney and his gang always walk away with a huge chunk of change. There is no down side for them. So when GM and Chrysler were on the ropes Romney famously wrote in the New York Times "Let Detroit go Bankrupt." By that he meant a restructuring *à la Bain*, that is, figure out the maximum profit potential for the equity stakeholders. Except that in this case there were no takers. Not even Bain was willing to risk a dime on the industry that made America the powerhouse of the world. Nothing, nada, zilch. So very much against his Republican instincts, President Bush initiated a restructuring using public funds, an effort President Obama saw to its final (and successful) conclusion. Not only was the Romney formula doomed to failure, but now the Republican presumptive candidate has the audacity to claim credit for both Bush's and Obama's successful rescue of the auto industry. That is a new definition of the word *chutzpah*.

Lest people think that all equity capitalists are the same, lets look at another firm: Second Avenue Partners. First, their public statement:

"Second Avenue Partners is a Seattle-based provider of management, strategy, and capital for early stage companies. The partners invest their own money, typically directed at emerging Internet businesses in the high-tech field. Second Avenue Partners' investment approach is to make early-stage investments in promising ventures and build long-term relationships, actively assisting its portfolio companies in becoming market leaders."

OK, to be fair, their goal does not explicitly say anything about job creation either, but it does have a different tone altogether. Gone are references that the business is all about maximizing profit potential. Rather, it seems that helping companies succeed is the main objective. A real treat is to listen to the CEO himself, Nick Hanauer.[3] See if you can distinguish the difference between this equity capitalist and Mitt Romney. This guy is as far from Romney as you can get and yet he is in the same business and also a member of the almost mythical 1%. So the problem is not with equity capitalists in general, but as Governor Rick Perry told Fox News Channel's Sean Hannity, "There's a real difference between venture capitalism and vulture capitalism...Venture capitalism we like. Vulture capitalism, no. And the fact of the matter is that he's going to have to face up to this at some time or another, and South Carolina is as good a place to draw that line in the sand as any."

In a rare act of candor, Mr. Perry explained the difference between the venture capitalism that Mr. Hanauer and others like

---

3   You can see Hanauer's speech on You Tube: http://www.youtube.com/watch?v=sdZzgN4SInU

him practice and the "vulture" capitalism that Mitt Romney practices. The real dark secret Romney is hiding from all of us is that rich folks are not job creators. The job creators are the rest of us. Just ask a real venture capitalist.

May 18, 2012

The Reverend Wright Digression

God's wrath comes about because God's holiness and love have been violated by the sinfulness of man. Human beings who live their lives apart from God are really antagonistic towards and hateful of his way. This means people living in such estrangement are actually the enemies of God. Since mankind assaults everything good and pure that God is and stands for, he cannot but be in opposition to man's way. This holy and loving opposition to sinfulness in every form is called "God's wrath."[4]

This simple statement is a core belief of many in the Jewish, Muslim, and Christian faiths. Not all Christians subscribe to this view of the Divine but there are many churches and many pastors in America who do. They all have their special take, some more dramatic than others. Some preachers have a flamboyant style. Jeremiah Wright has a particular style that is more typical in black evangelical churches, but there are many white evangelicals, especially in the South, with similar colorful deliveries. Beyond the delivery, the idea that God punishes sinners in dramatic fashion is rooted in Scripture. The obvious reference is Noah's story where God was so upset with the world

---

4 Grace Communion International [http://www.gci.org/God/wrath]

that He wiped out every living creature saving only a pair of each so as to start all over again.

Preachers famous and not-so-famous invoke God's wrath on any number of subjects. Reverend Pat Robertson, when the city of Dover, Pennsylvania voted out the school board that had imposed "intelligent design" on the school curriculum, famously said, *"I'd like to say to the good citizens of Dover: If there is a disaster in your area, don't turn to God, you just rejected him from your city. And don't wonder why he hasn't helped you when problems begin, if they begin. I'm not saying they will, but if they do, just remember, you just voted God out of your city. And if that's the case, don't ask for his help because he might not be there."* That was a clear message to Dover that God would be not be inclined to help that city, although Robertson wasn't sure what exactly He would do. Robertson was to make a similar threat to Orlando, Florida when Disney World decided to have a "gay day" at that famous amusement park. He went on, *"I would warn Orlando that you're right in the way of some serious hurricanes, and I don't think I'd be waving those flags in God's face if I were you, This is not a message of hate – this is a message of redemption. But a condition like this will bring about the destruction of your nation. It'll bring about terrorist bombs; it'll bring earthquakes, tornadoes, and possibly a meteor."* This time Robertson was more specific with his threats, and interestingly he also threw in the entire country for good measure. Apparently, Orlando was important enough that it could cause all of us to be threatened. What is equally fascinating was his choice of words. He favored "your nation" to "our nation." Robertson, who fancies himself a political figure as well and who actually ran for the Presidency of the United States, referred to his country as "your country" preferring not to be associated with its sinfulness.

The case of hurricane Katrina is intriguing in that all three religions, Christianity, Islam, and Judaism, had representatives with their own explanations for God's revenge on sorrowful New Orleans. The folks of al-Qa'ida in Iraq had the simplest thought, that *"God attacked America, and the prayers of the oppressed were answered."* They seemed to have taken quite a bit into consideration. A Jewish Rabbi, on the other hand, was much more specific. Ovadia Yosef, a prominent ultra-Orthodox Israeli rabbi, declared Hurricane Katrina to be *"God's punishment for President Bush's support of the August 2005 withdrawal of Jewish settlers from the Gaza strip."* The good Rabbi clearly has special insights on God's Jewish side.

The Christian statements were a bit more varied, however. Gerhard Maria Wagner, briefly an auxiliary bishop of Linz, attributed Hurricane Katrina to God's ire caused by the town's reputation for lax sexual behavior, claiming that the hurricane destroyed brothels, nightclubs and abortion clinics: *"It's no coincidence that in New Orleans all five abortion clinics as well as night clubs were destroyed."* The good Bishop made sure he included a number of sins. It is interesting that he lumped nightclubs in with abortion clinics and threw in brothels for good measure, covering all the bases as it were. American evangelist John Hagee's slightly different take linked the hurricane to a gay pride event known as "Southern Decadence Day", which was to have been held in the town's French Quarter a few days after the hurricane hit. He said in 2006, *"I believe that New Orleans had a level of sin that was offensive to God, and they are — were — recipients of the judgment of God for that. The newspaper carried the story in our local area, that was not carried nationally, that there was to be a homosexual parade there on the Monday that the Katrina came."* Hagee who has a track record of making outlandish statements, many of which he had to apologize for, concentrated his focus on the gays as the explanation for Katrina. All three religions were represented in the "wrath of God" against New Orleans, but I have to say that the Christians were the most creative and diverse, it turns out. Well, the myth of a large Christian conspiracy can be dispelled because even among the believers in God's retribution for sinfulness, there seems to be little agreement as to the causes.

Homosexuality is also a persistent obsession among the "God's wrath" believers. As the late Reverend Jerry Falwell explained, *"AIDS is the wrath of a just God against homosexuals. To oppose it would be like an Israelite jumping in the Red Sea to save one of Pharaoh's charioteers ... AIDS is not just God's punishment for homosexuals; it is God's punishment for the society that tolerates homosexuals."* This particular twist, of course, is the explanation for a disease, which incidentally was not really caused by homosexual behavior, but unfortunately for them spread like wildfire among the gay community due to their proclivities for unprotected sex. I wonder what the good Reverend would say to the millions of non-gay Africans afflicted by this horrible disease. I'm sure he would have a ready made explanation for that.

So in face of all that, is it a big surprise that the evangelical Christian Reverend Wright would find a Godly explanation for the "chickens coming home to roost" in America after so much sin has been perpetuated by our previous governments? Ironically, Reverend Wright was inspired by an American Ambassador being interviewed on Fox News, who used the "chickens" remark to explain what he thought was going on with the 9/11 attacks. (And before people accuse me of supporting Reverend Wright's outlandish beliefs, I make clear here and now that I do not support the Reverend's characterizations of why the terrorists attacked America on 9/11.) Still, he is hardly the only one blaming America. Jerry Falwell and Pat Robertson came to the same conclusion as Wright but from an entirely different direction. Falwell explicitly said, *"What we saw on Tuesday as terrible as it is could be minuscule if in fact God continues to lift the curtain and allow the enemies of America to give us probably what we deserve."* Included here are the videos of the Reverends.[5] Please note that the remarks made by Falwell and Robertson were made during a TV interview format whilst Wright's remarks were part of a fiery sermon delivered to parishioners in church.

And that is the main point: in church. What Wright did is as common as apple pie in today's evangelical churches. This particular style of "fire and brimstone" preaching is not prevalent in all evangelical churches, but it is quite familiar. There are preachers who frequently invoke God and His capacity to punish sin in apocalyptic fashion. Preachers have different styles

---

5   http://www.youtube.com/watch?v=kMkBgA9_oQ4

and chose different types of sin they wish to inveigh against but the gist is the same. The messages are very similar. God will punish the wicked in some sort of obvious fashion, either with natural disasters, man-made disasters, or even disease.

Personally, I have no use for any of it. Whether they are left-wing grievances or right-wing grievances I don't believe God goes out of His way to create disasters in which innocent lives are extinguished. I don't believe God is in the business of promoting "snuff films" to teach humans moral lessons. But many people do believe in such things. To single out Reverend Wright as a particular heinous character is disingenuous at best and often is just a convenient shorthand to slander the President. Bringing back Reverend Wright (again) in the context of another Presidential campaign is an insult to our democracy and it is hypocrisy writ large. Religious leaders use hyperbole in church to make their points. It is their stock in trade. To his credit, Reverend Wright confines his remarks to his pulpit where they belong and aimed them at his parishioners unlike so many other preachers who make their intemperate remarks to the rest of us while pretending they are neither political pundits nor politicians.

May 23, 2012

The Lessons of the Walker Recall

"Money talks; Bullshit walks."

- American proverb

Americans have some quaint and colorful sayings, some of them very earthy. In the case of the singular recall election in Wisconsin yesterday, this is one case where American popular wisdom seems to have prevailed.

Because of the complexity of the funding for this recall election the numbers vary depending on how you count. There was money spent on media advertising, organization, consultants, and so much more. Most fair pundits put the estimated funding discrepancy between Governor Scott Walker and Mayor Tom Barrett ranging from 7-1 in favor of Walker to10-1. The latest figures I have seen show approximately $40 million spent on Walker's campaign and $4 million spent on Barrett's campaign.

Whatever the actual final numbers will be, one thing is fairly clear. The Supreme Court ruling on the *Citizen's United* case has unleashed unlimited funds from the corporate sector and independent billionaires intent on influencing elections. The most disturbing aspect of this new legal experiment is that much of this money is donated anonymously.

One of the lessons learned from this unusual election is that it is hard to know with any precision what role big money played in Wisconsin's election. Still, it is not unreasonable to assume that money played some role. There are many factors that went into the Walker victory, the main non-partisan point being that many voters did not think recall elections should be used for anything other than for criminal wrongdoing. Although there is vast discontent with Walker's policies in Wisconsin, Americans by and large are strong believers in fairness and don't usually support unusual remedies to remove politicians from office. The classic case, of course, is Bill Clinton's Monica Lewinsky scandal which left Americans with a bad taste throughout the country, but resulted in the impeachment attempt by a partisan Republican Party being rejected by a country tired of the overreaching by the opposition.

It could be said that the opposition to Governor Walker over-reached, that the recall remedy was more than the public wanted. Perhaps the public would have settled for a reprimand, but our system does not really allow for that so a recall election is one of the few ways the public can register their disapproval.

However, it is dangerous to read too much into this election. Yes, it is true that the unions in Wisconsin were not successful in removing their Governor from office in a special election. That is the bottom line and one cannot underplay that. But beyond that, it is not very clear what are the main consequences of this election. Not as reported, however, is the real possibility that the Wisconsin Senate is likely to go back into the the hands of Democrats, giving Walker a setback he did not get from his personal recall election. The recall will likely turn the Senate from a Republican majority to a Democratic majority, a major defeat for Walker's agenda.

It will be interesting to see if Walker will continue his onslaught on Wisconsin's middle class. Although prognostications are always dangerous, it seems that Walker might become a bit more humble in his approach to governing and the legislature in Wisconsin will be more balanced as a result of all the recall efforts. After all, most Americans wish for a more balanced approach to government and generally reject all the hyper-partisanship that has become the norm in Washington D.C. these days.

Governor Walker would be well served if he does not allow his victory go to his head and believe that he now has *carte blanche* to pursue a right-wing agenda. That would be a big misreading of the electoral results. Governor Walker has been given a second chance but a most telling number is that a full 60% of the voters in Wisconsin believe that their Governors should only be recalled or impeached for serious misconduct and policy differences do not really qualify.

One thing seems clear, however, that there is too much unaccountable money in politics as a result of the *Citizens United* Supreme Court decision. Mitt Romney took advantage of this new law to overwhelm his competition for the Republican nomination. He obliterated competitors like Rick Santorum and Newt

Gingrich with massive TV advertising subsidized by unlimited spending by mostly anonymous billionaires. This is an issue that will not go away soon.

America has to decide whether a few billionaires should have special rights due to their financial position. Is money really the same as speech? Are Corporations really people? Aside from being the name of this blog, this is a question that will haunt America for the foreseeable future.

June 6, 2012

The Great Gas Gambit

All those people who predicted gas prices would be over five dollars a gallon this summer must all apologize to the American people.

Now.

That includes most of the leaders of the Republican Party who were all so happy that gas prices were climbing a few months ago so they could blame the President for one more thing. Senate Minority Leader Mitch McConnell went so far as saying, "This President will go to any length to drive up gas prices and pave the way for his ideological agenda." Really, Mitch? And what agenda would that be? Ensuring his defeat in November? Making his fellow citizens as miserable as possible? Ensuring that ordinary Americans would have less money to pay for food? I wonder which ideological agenda Mitch is talking about because, of course, the good senator from Kentucky did not elaborate or fully explain the details.

It seemed, for a while, that Republicans and their boosters at Fox News and other assorted right-wing outlets couldn't stop talking about how gas prices were going to skyrocket during the summer based on their vast knowledge of economics.

We can excuse the usual fellow travelers like Limbaugh, Beck, and Hannity, for their underprivileged education and little understanding of how the real world works. After all, they are entertainers, so we shouldn't expect people who are colleagues of Ozzie Osborne to have any special knowledge of the dynamics of commodities fluctuations. Nobody in his right mind would go to the Beiber for economics advice. Let the Beiber be Beiber, and the rest of us should try and get our information from people who know a little bit more about international markets.

But wait a minute! Isn't Mitt Romney an expert about markets? Or so he says. Just ask him on the campaign trail and he will tell you that he is not really a politician; he is a business man. A very savvy business man with oodles and oodles of experience with capital formation, markets, and all those complicated things about which the Minority Leader is so ignorant about. At least, the clueless McConnell is not running for President, and he is barely mentioned as a choice for Vice President so we have to give ole' Mitch a pass. After all, he just has to convince the good people of Kentucky he knows what he is talking about, voters who might be brighter than he thinks.

And exactly what is Romney's excuse? I recall he too joined the Republican bandwagon and was quite critical of the President's policies which he squarely blamed for the rising gas prices. With Romney's vast knowledge of the economy he would fix all that he alleged. He didn't quite go as far as the quasi-genius Gingrich who had a secret plan to bring gas prices down to two dollars or so. But the businessman Romney was quick to point out the

President was responsible for the rise in gas prices and that under his (Romney's) capable administration such calamities were just not going to happen because of his great command of economics, the markets, capital formation, and so on and so on.

So Mitt, where is your apology?

You see, I don't believe Romney, McConnell and these other gentlemen should apologize for being wrong. I mean, we all make mistakes. My biggest mistake was believing that Ronald Reagan would not win a second term. If it weren't for his fellow Republicans hating FDR so much and passing a law prohibiting presidents from having more than two terms, Reagan might have won a third term – that's how wrong I was. And I never apologized either because I never claimed to be an expert prognosticator. But Romney claims knowledge of economics and especially knowledge of how markets work. Heck, his whole campaign is predicated on the principle that his special knowledge as a businessman would enable him to turn around our economy. It's, if you pardon my French, his *raison d' être*.

So yes, Mitt, when you get gas prices wrong, you have to apologize to the American people. Not for being wrong, but for pretending you know things that you don't know much about. For perpetuating a hoax on the people. For lying about your capacity to understand how markets work when in reality you are no better than Justin Beiber at economics. And maybe just a little bit better than Ozzie Osbourne. Just maybe.

June 27, 2012

The Dysfunction Myth

Democracy is not pretty to look at. It's messy. It was always messy from the very formation of the United States. The Founding Fathers argued about everything but ended up with great compromises like the Declaration of Independence and the Constitution.

And now we have the Affordable Care Act, a badly needed beginning of healthcare reform almost one hundred years in the making.

Underscoring this historical moment is the myth of American dysfunctionality. Every major accomplishment has been fought tooth and nail and that is when statesmen step up to the plate. Jefferson, Lincoln, Roosevelt, JFK, and LBJ were among the many who moved the ball forward. Too early to say about Obama, but in the case of healthcare reform the statesman this time around is Chief Justice John Roberts.

Roberts confounded everybody. The Liberals thought he was a lost cause, a hopeless partisan in the same league as the most partisan Justice on the Supreme Court, Antonin Scalia. But the Liberals were wrong. When Roberts famously said, "My job is to call balls and strikes and not to pitch or bat," many Liberals did not really believe him. Since he was appointed by a Republican

President, the nefarious George W., it was feared he was bound to be another partisan judge like Scalia, Alito, and Thomas. But something mysterious usually happens on the way to powerful positions. People become more realistic and more importantly, more *responsible*. It is one thing to be on the outside, throwing rocks; it is another thing to accept a position of great responsibility and have the fate of one's fellow citizens in one's hands.

Conservatives also got Roberts wrong, much like they did Earl Warren. Conservatives thought that Roberts was going to be a "team player" and play for their team regardless of what was in the interest of the Nation. But Roberts surprised the Conservatives too. We may never know what Roberts' personal view of the Affordable Care Act (Obamacare) is, but that does not matter because he correctly understood that his job is to find a way to validate the will of Congress and the President.

Predictably, the right-wing noise machine is going to go into overdrive and badmouth Justice Roberts. They will call him traitor and worse. There will undoubtedly be calls for his impeachment from the Tea Party types and their sycophants. These extreme ideologues claim to be patriots but do not really understand how our country works, how democracy works, or even what the meaning of the Constitution is. Then there will be the inevitable conspiracy theories, casting Roberts as a stooge or an evil genius. There will be much cynicism spread because so many of us cannot believe that honorable men still exist.

America has much to celebrate. Not only has healthcare taken a big step forward, but the political system has been proven to work as the Founders intended. Justice Roberts showed us all that he has a deep understanding of American history, that he understands the great responsibility that comes with being Chief Justice of the Supreme Court, that it is not a trivial job for trivial people. That he, along with the President, does not have the luxury of letting his emotions get the better of him. That he is not part of some ideological "side" which if it doesn't get its way will stamp its feet like a three-year old. No, Roberts showed us that along with Obama, he was one of the few adults in the room and rose to the occasion.

This is the stuff of history! It is not the time to play a sleazy game to get a great headline in the Drudge Report or praise from the professional bloviators. This is America at its finest, when people from different backgrounds, different philosophies come together for the benefit of all of the American people. It is so rare these days that too many people will miss it, which is why it deserves a special mention.

And, to paraphrase the great Mark Twain, "Reports of the death of American democracy are greatly exaggerated."

June 28, 2012

Malicious Kook Power

Definition of KOOK
: one whose ideas or actions are eccentric, fantastic, or insane :
Definition of MALICE
1: desire to cause pain, injury, or distress to another
2: intent to commit an unlawful act or cause harm without legal justification or excuse

- Merriam-Webster

Who would have thought that the likes of Michele Bachmann, Glen Beck, and Rush Limbaugh would have so much influence in the Middle East? These three and others like them continue to be national embarrassments and have little influence in their own country outside of their rabid group of fans, but in faraway Egypt, of all places, their antics have provoked otherwise level-headed people to believe the preposterous lie that America had a secret agenda to support the Muslim Brotherhood in the Egyptian elections.

And where did they unearth such an obvious lie?

It all started with Congresswoman (and ex-candidate for President) Michele Bachmann's allegation that the US Congress has been penetrated by the Muslim Brotherhood. Not content with this simple baseless allegation, Bachmann goes all in with this whopper: "It appears that there has been deep penetration in the halls of our United States government by the Muslim Brotherhood," Bachmann told radio host Sandy Rios in June. "It appears that there are individuals who are associated with the Muslim Brotherhood who have positions, very sensitive positions, in our Department of Justice, our Department of Homeland Security, potentially even in the National Intelligence Agency." Words worthy of Senator Joe McCarthy himself.

Nobody in his right mind pays much attention to these obvious cries for attention as the media, generally speaking, does little to report on this nonsense, but these malicious kooky ideas do find their way into the blogosphere, particularly through the right-wing "ditto-heads" who are all too happy to promote the most preposterous lies about our President and his administration.

Not to be outdone, Glen Beck has been advancing some pretty paranoid scenarios of his own. The enclosed video clip[6] tells the story in chilling detail, it tells a tale that should frighten us all. Beck manages to assemble a a group of "experts" who sound very rational, discussing the demise of the United States at the hands of the Muslim Brotherhood, even implicating the President of the United States in a ridiculous plot working with elements of the Muslim Brotherhood to obliterate our country as we know it. Gone is the bombast Beck exhibited at Fox News, the bombast he thrilled Rupert Murdoch with because it ginned up ratings, fattening both of their wallets in the process. (When Beck's over the top shtick stopped bringing in the big bucks, ol' Rupert, always the sentimental one, dropped Glen like a hot potato.) But here, the soft spoken Beck with his ever so calm

---

6   http://www.youtube.com/watch?v=7BEyf6pPdyc

guests weave a tale that is worthy of the Syfy channel except that gullible listeners in Egypt were apparently tuned in.

Finally, of course, there is the always reliable *über*-malicious kook himself, Rush Limbaugh who completes the puzzle with this gem:

Huma Abedin, Mrs. Anthony Weiner, Mrs. Huma Weiner, she is Hillary Clinton's number one aide. And Huma's mother is best friends with the new First Lady of Egypt, the wife of the new Muslim Brotherhood guy, Morsi. That's really all you need to know. But there's much more to know. That's why Hillary is out celebrating the brotherhood. That's why Hillary is joining Obama in telling the military to give it up for the Brotherhood guy. Because Huma's mom, there's actually a group, the Muslim Sisterhood, essentially, that is an offshoot of the Brotherhood. And Huma's mom is best friends with the new so-called First Lady of Egypt, who is also a member of the Sisterhood. Folks, it's Peyton place. It's too much to keep up with.

As Limbaugh boldly states, there's more, much more (including the the omitted fact that Weiner is a Jew), but this modest article is not about detailing all the sordid particulars of the paranoid delusions of America's malicious kooks. That is more print than any of them deserve. Those of you who are fascinated with the ranting of the professional paranoids, feel free to investigate on your own. There's plenty more.

However, there is a larger point to be made. The antics of those many of us regard as kooks, or entertainment as some will, are taken seriously abroad by too many people. The spectacle of our

Secretary of State, Hillary Clinton being pelted by tomatoes and jeered in Egypt is not just a humiliation she does not deserve. It is a humiliation of our President (who incidentally, in spite of vicious rumors to the contrary, does not deserve this either). Most importantly, it is a humiliation directed at the United States of America – that is – us American citizens. All due to the antics of our fellow kooky citizens who amuse themselves by slandering our country for fun and profit.

And where is the "never apologize for America" Mitt Romney in all this? Why is Mr. Romney not rising to defend his country? Or at least being so bold as to denounce the malicious kooks in his own party? It is not enough to dismiss the eminently dismissible Sarah Palin who is a bastion of reason compared with these three. Romney wants us to believe he will be a bold leader defending America abroad when he cannot even muster the courage to defend America from her enemies within.

At great risk of sounding anti-free enterprise, at what point does this type of behavior become seditious? Just asking.

PS Since this article was published Senator John McCain made an passionate defense of Huma Abedin on the Senate floor. If only Romney had half the courage of John McCain he might get half his votes.

July 18, 2012

The Ugly American

Most Americans only get interested in foreign policy when either a) someone bombs us or b) we bomb someone. I realize this is a bit of oversimplification but the average American is just not interested in world affairs or the fact that as the world's super-power, we have daily dealings with countries and people across the entire globe. Americans just don't think that our presence in the world is all that important.

Of course, that changes from time to time as when the Olympic Games roll around and all of a sudden our competitive juices get revved up. Suddenly it matters a lot that a small group of female gymnasts besting all the world's other gymnasts becomes all-consuming and all-important. There are other times, on smaller scales, when Americans care about what happens in the world, but on the whole, the average American is not terribly interested or informed about world events.

However, our presence in the world matters. A lot. America has commercial interests all over the world and not just limited to oil or iPod sales, to name two obvious concerns. America is a true world leader and whether we care or not, the whole world looks to America for leadership.

Which is why Mitt Romney's uninspired tour of three of the most American-friendly nations, Great Britain, Israel, and Poland does not bode well for the Republican prospect. The press has had its fun with the many gaffes and missteps by both the presidential candidate himself and his closest aides, but the whole is more important than its parts. Sure, blaring headlines in the London papers announcing, "Mitt the Twit" are not helpful, but the image of a would be world leader incapable of navigating friendly waters should give Americans pause.

More egregious, however, was Romney's blatant disregard of the delicate and tricky role America plays in the Middle East. In his zeal to contrast himself with President Obama, shore up support with Jewish voters back home, and assist his unquenchable thirst for campaign cash, he threw caution to the wind by adopting an uncompromising pro-Israeli government stand. I say Israeli government because his chummy relationship with Bibi Netanyahu, the current Prime Minister should not be confused with a pro-Israel position. Netanyahu represents a conservative government, which in a parliamentary democracy such as Israel could change in a blink of an eye.

Much more important is the delicate balance America has to achieve between being a supporter of Israel the country and its true interests, while maintaining a position as an honest broker between the Israelis and the Palestinians. Maybe posturing with his buddy Bibi will score him points back home with the yahoos and fool some Jewish voters into believing Romney has Israel's back, but Israel is not simply defined by its current government and its current policies. Israel is a complex democratic society similar to ours with many points of view and it is clearly in the country's interest to co-exist peacefully with its Arab neighbors. Putting down Palestinian "culture" as Romney did does not help Israel in any way.

Every American President, liberal or conservative, understands this delicate balancing act and none has ever lowered himself to being merely a blatant cheerleader for Israel. Most Israelis understand this simple fact. By ignoring the true interests of the Israeli people in order to score cheap campaign points, Romney is not only showing his lack of mastery of the complex art of diplomacy, but also putting his immediate personal needs ahead of Israel. Jewish voters should not be fooled.

So far, the most under-reported story of Romney's latest international tour is his shameless fund-raising on foreign soil yet the press reported his ability to raise millions from foreigners in the most nonchalant way. Is is not enough that the Citizen's United Supreme Court decision opened the floodgates of money pouring into our elections? The Supreme Court declared that corporations are equivalent to people and as citizens have the right to donate money to influence elections, in unlimited ways and in secret. That is a travesty that the Congress is trying to address, but since when is it OK for foreign interests – big foreign interests – to participate in our elections with cash? Where is the outrage from the people who are trying to make voting in elections as difficult as possible in order to prevent foreigners from voting? I think everybody agrees that foreigners voting in our elections is a no-no, but how about foreigners giving cash to presidential candidates? Are we so *blasé* and cynical that raising millions abroad hardly raises an eyebrow? If a handful of illegal immigrants voting in our elections is supposedly a travesty so terrible that we are willing to thwart American citizens from voting in order to prevent that possibility, how can we ignore millions in foreign cash finding its way to political candidates? I am reasonably confidant that Romney broke no laws when he collected millions overseas. I don't believe he is careless enough to openly break the law. But, one might ask, how is it possible that foreigners could legally influence our elections with cash and what does this say about a candidate willing to take large sums from foreigners?

Romney supporters like to say that his trip abroad was a resounding success. I guess it all depends on what his goals were. Based on the results, we can be confident in assuming that foreign policy was not his main priority.

August 1, 2012

America's Decline?

After watching the Olympic Games on TV it is hard to conclude that America is in decline. If it is, somebody forgot to tell our young Olympian athletes. Watching them perform was a treat that every American should have savored. From the hard-boiled professionals of the NBA to the pre-collegiate athletes like our female gymnasts, they all showed us what talent, dedication, and hard work can accomplish. Only the mega-sized Chinese athletes, a product of a Soviet-style massive government program, came even close in medal count to the Americans.

Except the Americans are not part of a gigantic government experiment, much to the chagrin of the conservative critique of contemporary America. President Obama has not turned the Olympic movement into another government project. He clearly has no intention to. There are some who delude themselves into thinking that our President is actively conspiring to turn our country into an oppressive central government-run state even as there is little evidence of that. Our Olympic athletes are a product of the best America has to offer: privately run professional leagues, collegiate organized sports, public and private school organized sports, with a smattering of diehard individuals perfecting their special talents. No centralized control necessary because freedom, combined with a strong work ethic and a strong desire to succeed is all we need.

Our Olympic athletes embody the best of America, something that has not changed since the first Olympiad of the modern era in 1896.

During the Cold War there were the titanic struggles between the US and Soviet Union, which used the power of its massive government to create a program designed to foster its image as a super power. The Soviets used the Olympics to show the world they were at the same level or better than the dreaded capitalistic flag bearer that was the United States. For them the Olympics was just an extension of their foreign policy much like the Chinese today. They have emulated the West in just about everything except their version of the Olympics which is a carbon copy of the old Soviet system.

America stood fast during the Cold War, preferring to stick to its ideals of personal liberty even when it was tempting to opt for a massive government program to promote success at the Games watched by the entire world.

The Olympic revival, starting with the 1896 games in Athens, Greece, was conceived by Baron Pierre de Coubertin and was initially an all-male affair. Coubertin's vision was that nationalism would play a minor role and that only amateurs would participate. The Games have greatly expanded since then and the ideal of minimizing nationalism has all but evaporated, even though there is no official mention of which country "won" the

Games. However, the daily medal counts reports belie the spirit of anti-chauvinism, although only China has a serious government program (along with a few diehard communist countries like Cuba and North Korea).

Every country on the planet takes pride in the successes of their compatriots, including the USA, which proves that there is no need for the government to be involved to produce a sense of patriotism.

Judging by the performance of our athletes in London, it is difficult to make the argument that the United States is a country in decline, that our values of self-reliance, hard work, and success-oriented behavior are compromised. Our young people are still the envy of the world.

I always suspected that most of the hand-wringing about America's decline as a country and a culture has a mostly political agenda behind it. There are people with a vested interest in accusing our President of curtailing our Constitutional freedoms, and adopting a "statist" style of governance which in turn is leading us down a ruinous path. No matter that there is little truth to this assertion and the best example the President's critics can come up with is his health care reforms which are based on a private sector model and not a "government takeover" model as is falsely alleged.

If you believe the President is a closet Socialist, hell-bent on eroding our freedoms, turning our government into a gigantic leviathan that will control every aspect of our lives, then I have to admit he has been a colossal failure.

But if you believe the President is a democratic reformer working within the limits of our Constitution, who represents the best of our country, then I believe he has been largely successful.

Our Olympic athletes surely represent the best our country has to offer and they have shown the world that American values are alive. America is hardly in decline. You can even make the assertion that American values and America itself is as strong as ever.

We have a lot to be proud of and thankful for.

August 13, 2012

Ryan's Medicare Problem

In the point, counter-point world of campaigns, much is lost in the hyperbole and obsession over details. Most issues are not black and white, so to reduce them to slogans based on one esoteric point over another, doesn't give voters a chance to properly evaluate the competing claims.

The Medicare debate is particularly complicated because it involves scores of factors, many of which are difficult to control. Most slogans actually say very little that is useful to the voter. "End Medicare as we know it" is a truism that says nothing just as "government takeover of healthcare" is a falsehood that doesn't provide any information. The first slogan, used by Democrats, is true but meaningless. It tells us nothing about what the Republicans are up to. Its intention is to scare people afraid of change, nothing more. It actually begs the question as to whether the Republican changes to Medicare are an improvement or not, thereby shutting down any effective debate. "Government takeover of healthcare" is a slogan used by Republicans to denigrate "Obamacare" (the Affordable Care Act) which not only is a falsehood, since the ACA is actually a reform of the already existing private health insurance system, but equally shuts off debate by scaring voters into believing that the President is a closest Socialist hell bent on turning America into a big gulag.

So what then happens is the commentary class then will go into excruciating detail trying to unravel a most complex issue that requires reams of documents to explain. The result is that the public is as confused as ever, not knowing who or what to believe.

The intent of this piece is not to be an exhaustive analysis of the issues but to make a few observations as to what the philosophies are behind the various reforms. It is really up to the individual voter to read as much as possible about the various plans and their critics and come to his or her own conclusion.

However, as one who leans towards the liberal side of the equation I cannot help but notice that Mr. Ryan's Medicare reforms, where he wants to weed seniors away from the admittedly government-run current system to a private insurance based system much like the rest of us have, has the peculiarity of being reliant on the success of the President's Affordable Care Act. An interesting twist since his partner, Mitt Romney, is staking his candidacy in large measure on the repeal of ACA. I predict that if Mr. Romney is elected president, repealing ACA will be his first official flip-flop since he will find out it will not be easy to unravel such a large piece of legislation whose many individual parts are more popular than the whole. In a word, he will find out, as President Obama did, the power of the filibuster rule (in the case the Democrats should lose the Senate) or the power of the Senate (should the Democrats remain in the majority).

But the problems for Ryan don't end there. There is a real dif-ference in philosophy between the two major parties and in particular between the Obama/Biden and the Romney/Ryan teams. The President is all about spreading the risk among all Americans. Unlike the caricature of his "spreading the wealth," he genuinely believes that 1) all Americans should have medical insurance regardless of income level and 2) a single risk pool should be the strength of the American people as a whole. One can disagree with this philosophy, but that is what the man believes in.

The private insurance businesses, however, believe in creating risk pool groups. This is how they manage their business. Lower risk groups, therefore, pay the lowest premiums and the higher risk groups pay increasingly higher premiums because their risk is higher. It makes perfect sense as a business model which is why the business minded Romney and Ryan support this type of approach. This is what they call the free market.

The problem with this free market approach to human services is that, although great for business, it is not so great for people who end up sick and old. The free market is a wonderful mechanism to deliver most goods and services. No one has come up with a better economic system that is more innovative, nimble, and efficient. But healthcare is in a different class. One might even say it is in a unique class because as we all get old we all use healthcare disproportionately. Young, healthy people rarely need medical intervention unless they get involved in a catastrophic accident or contract an unpredictable disease. Consequently, as a group they are in a rather low risk pool.

So here's where the differences in philosophies clash. By insisting that everybody is in the same boat, the President is telling younger people that they should pay more now in insurance in order to have a guarantee that they won't pay significantly more when they get old. That is the bargain that Obama would like to see for America. The Republican alternative (when you get deep in the weeds with Ryan's reforms) is to rely on the private sector for seniors. This means, of course, they will get caught up in increasingly higher and more expensive risk pools. To his credit, Ryan left the public option open for seniors – after howls of protest from Democrats and senior groups like AARP – but all that will accomplish is to push the really sick into the government plan, making it even more expensive than it is now. Ironically, it is Obama's cost saving ACA that can palliate the effect somewhat. No matter what, though, the highest risk people will cost the most, because the population as whole was treated unequally to start with.

People who see the market as some sort of religion that has to be correct for everything will embrace the Republican philosophy until it will be too late if they find themselves out of luck. We have been living in a mixed economy for some time now. We have maintained a market economy that works well (with a few exceptions) but have also embraced government intervention in certain areas of common good. Most Republicans have accepted that the free market in its purest form cannot meet all of people's needs. Services like fire, police, public works, primary and secondary education, have been in public hands for a long time and although not without problems, are considered by most best done through a public service, not private enterprise. Nobody in his right mind would suggest we turn the fire departments into a private insurance scheme where premiums are optional and varied. And if you chose not to participate, well, your house will just burn down as the fire department would limit itself to protecting those who paid their insurance premiums.

Healthcare is not very different from protection against fire. We all need it. It is not an "option" unless you are so heartless as to think people should be allowed to die at the scene of an accident or from a curable disease. Fortunately, very few people think that.

There is much to reform in healthcare. The costs are too high. There are many inefficiencies in the system. There is too much corruption. The list is quite long. All ideas that contribute towards solving these problems should be welcomed, and it should not matter who comes up with them. But America has a choice to make. Should the private insurance companies be allowed to make up the rules that satisfy their bottom line? Or should the public sector create rules that are in everyone's interest that take into account that as we grow older our needs are greater and costs are higher? Are we all in this together? Or should each group be forced into fending for itself?

August 22, 2012

Dirty Harry Meets Harvey

Film buffs remember Jimmy Stewart's iconic portrayal of a simple man who had a six foot two invisible rabbit as a friend. Stewart carried the 1950 film classic, *Harvey* which centered around the question of whether Jimmy Stewart's character was sane or insane.

There is no question that the rambling Clint Eastwood is sane. His performance at the Republican National Convention, where he conversed with an invisible Barack Obama, may have been a bit bizarre but it nicely encapsulated the fiction that continues to be the criticism of the President. Clint Eastwood was short on specifics, but he tried to reinforce the myth that the President is a nice guy but in over his head, that he is not up to the job.

The media generally has panned Eastwood's convention performance, alleging that he sounded like an "old," almost senile man who was generally an embarrassment and out of synch with the Republican convention. Certainly, he was a shadow of himself if you compare his performance in Tampa with the powerful Superbowl commercial he did for Chrysler. The Chrysler commercial was criticized by Republicans for sounding too pro-Obama. Somehow, truth-telling, which is what Eastwood was doing in the commercial, seems to benefit the President. But Eastwood went beyond truth-telling in that hard-hitting Dirty

Harry style spot. The commercial not only reminded Americans of the critical role the President had in saving the US automobile industry, but Clint made that all-American pitch, that we were merely at halftime, alluding to not only the break in the football game but also, some concluded, to the halfway mark of Obama's presidency. Therefore, it became imperative for the Republican Party to make clear to the voters that Eastwood was a supporter of the Republican ticket.

But Eastwood is no old senile man. Far from it. He is as clever as a fox. His performance was not only designed to pander to the delegates at the convention but was also designed to plant seeds of doubt among the undecided voters. Unfortunately for Clint, it was too clever by half and he got lost in his contradictions. It is hard to make the point that Obama is a "nice guy" who is in over his head while simultaneously attributing epithets such as "go fuck yourself" and "shut up" to him since most people think of their President as a mild-mannered man. Eastwood did, however, capture the essence of the Republican message and talking to a non-existent Obama pretty much says it all. The Romney/Ryan campaign is entirely dependent on perpetuating a critique of a non-existent Obama. The following is a small representative sample:

The Stimulus was a Failure

It is a classic fallacy that if something does not solve every problem it must have failed. In order to make this statement believable one must suspend all reality. The only legitimate critique is that the stimulus could have been larger, but that is counter to Republican orthodoxy that government is powerless to solve anything. Thousands of jobs were either saved or created. All manner of projects, both in the public sector and private, were brought to success. For example, Governor Rick Perry of Texas, would never have been able to balance his budget without stimulus funding. All manner of infrastructure work was accomplished in spite of a few projects which were not quite "shovel ready." The Republican critique only works if one concentrates on the few failures. A short quote from Energy.com tells a small part of the story:

> Today, the Obama Administration announced the selection of the first public-private pilot institute for manufacturing innovation in Youngstown, Ohio, to help revitalize American manufacturing and encourage companies to invest in the United States. This new partnership, the National Additive Manufacturing Innovation Institute (NAMII), was selected through a competitive process to receive an initial investment of $30 million in federal funding and matched by $40 million from the winning consortium of manufacturing firms, universities, community colleges, and non-profit organizations from the Ohio-Pennsylvania 'Tech Belt.' August 16, 2012[7]

There are countless initiatives that did not make the news. Unlike the simplistic slogans characterizing the media as "liberal," the media gravitate more to sensational stories. For example, the closing of a single plant such as Solyndra in California is simple to report, while telling the bigger story of NAMII (the National Additive Manufacturing Innovation Institute) is more complex and nuanced and therefore a more difficult story to tell in a five minute segment.

---

7   Department of Commerce

The Elimination of the Work Component of Welfare Myth

This blatant falsehood is essential to paint Obama as a protector of the shiftless and lazy class, complete with racial overtones since so many people assume that welfare recipients are mostly blacks. The best numbers available on welfare recipients: Black – 39.8%, White – 38.8%, Hispanic – 15.7%, Other – 3.3%, Asian – 2.4%.[8]

All the fact-checkers agree that Obama did not eliminate the work component for welfare recipients. He simply gave, within the provisions of the law, some flexibility to governors, such as Mitt Romney himself, regarding how to attain the work requirement. For a party that is constantly promoting states rights not only is this critique a lie but it is disingenuous as well as hypocritical.

The Gutting of Medicare Myth

This is clearly one of the most pernicious of all the Republican lies. The $716 billion number Republicans bandy about as "taking" from Medicare is really a tightening of the program by negotiating with hospitals and other providers smaller re-imbursements based on the expectations of an expanded population insured under the American Affordable Care Act (Obamacare). The Republicans, on the other hand, have made no secret of their desire to eliminate Medicare by forcing future seniors into the private insurance market with the promise of a

---

8   Answers.com

fixed subsidy that may or may not cover the insurance premiums, which will undoubtedly be extremely high based on probability factors. Ironically, only the full implementation of Obamacare with its insistence of insuring people with pre-existing conditions might palliate the Republican voucher plan. Of course, to add insult to injury, Ryan has the exact same cut to Medicare in his plan as Obama does.

Obama Believes Jobs Come from Government

This particular myth is actually quite easily disproved, although Republicans have repeatedly demonstrated that repeating a lie over and over again has an effect on the body politic. Public sector jobs grew by 4% under George W. Bush and shrank by 3% under Barack Obama, a fact that is just not generally known thanks to a failure of the Obama administration to push that point coupled with the media's infatuation with more sensationalist stories. Not only do too many people believe Obama is "growing" government but too many people don't realize he cut most of their taxes as well.

This is why Clint Eastwood's dialog with a non-existent Obama rings true. Critics have had a field day accusing President Obama of the most outrageous fantasies. The above examples are merely a few selected policy fabrications, but the concoctions have been many and varied. The smears on his reputation seem to be endless, from raising doubts about his own birth, his faith, his convictions, almost everything about him has been called into question – not as legitimate inquiry, but as deliberate fraudulent statements designed to misrepresent. The Republicans have been criticizing a non-existent Obama for years and getting away with it.

Clint indeed made their day.

September 5, 2012

Bopp 'til you Drop

James Bopp, is a rather obscure lawyer from Terre Haute, Indiana. I say obscure, because he is not known by the general public, but to the anti-abortion crowd he is kind of a hero. He has served as the general counsel for *National Right to Life* since 1978 and as the special counsel for *Focus on the Family* since 2004. Bopp was the editor of *Restoring the Right to Life: The Human Life Amendment.* (Provo: Brigham Young University Press, 1984)

This story is not, however, about Bopp's abortion *bona fides*. He is better known as the guy who brought us rivers of money to political campaigns as he argued successfully for *Citizens's United* in front of the Supreme Court.

His success had a improbable start. He was literally laughed out of court when he had the temerity to state that the hit piece on Hillary Clinton, *Hillary: The Movie*, was legitimate news and should be allowed to air on TV as would any news piece. The Federal Election Commission (FEC) told *Citizens United* that it couldn't air the film during primary season, because it amounted to a 90-minute campaign ad. In court, Bopp argued that the movie wasn't so different from what you'd see on *60 Minutes*, and its creators deserved First Amendment protections. At that point, US District Court Judge Royce Lamberth laughed out loud. "You can't compare this to *60 Minutes*," he said. "Did you read this transcript?"

But funnier things happened on the way to the Supreme Court since the justices saw fit to overturn the FEC's decision, thereby ushering in a new age of unlimited campaign spending whereby billionaires could contribute unlimited cash – anonymously if they wish – to support the candidates of their choice, virtually annihilating the years of campaign reforms that had been painstakingly achieved on a bipartisan basis over many years. One stroke of the pen eliminated years of legislative work. President Obama famously predicted that the decision would go down in history as a terrible experiment much to the visible disapproval of justice Alito during a State of the Union address.

The assumption, of course, by both Democrats and Republicans, was that the Republicans, with their billionaire minions would have a huge advantage and that cash advantage does seem to have materialized in that candidate Mitt Romney, the self-confessed candidate of the plutocrats, has been awash in campaign cash, much of it of dubious origin and difficult to account for. He used his cash advantage to blow away his Republican primary competition which is certainly evidence of poetic justice since Republicans generally welcomed the Supreme Court decision with open arms, not to mention open wallets. The Romney rivals never had a fighting chance as they were severely outspent by the *faux* conservative Romney and, in an ironic twist worthy of an Agatha Christie novel, the more conservative candidates were pulverized by the very money they worshiped, allowing the moderate and more "flexible" Romney to win the nomination. Never was the saying, "Be careful what you wish for..." more true.

Romney has demonstrated that the well-heeled are the ones in the best position to rake in the cash, not necessarily the ones with the most conservative ideas, which is why we have a Romney/Ryan ticket and not the converse. There is even loose talk among the conservative claque that Romney should step aside and allow for the ideologically more "pure" ticket of Ryan/Rubio.

But it is too late.

Romney, the poster child of unfettered capitalism, has won the money race fair and square under the new Bopp rules, and Bopp, as a modern Dr. Frankenstein, has joined his newly created monster who turns out to be exactly what the system created. He is an unfeeling money hound with no scruples or core principles aside from a strong desire to win at any cost, much like the mythical Gordon Gekko, that fictitious lizard of Wall Street fame.

The final irony is this. All that humongous horde of cash cannot hide the fact that Romney is a deeply flawed candidate and the instincts of the American people are proven correct once again. Romney is perceived as the phony he is by friend and foe alike. The only thing keeping his campaign even remotely competitive is that 1) there are people who genuinely dislike the President and would vote for Joe the Plumber before voting for Obama, and 2) the economy is in a sluggish recovery so therefore there is more pain out in the country than usual.

If it wasn't for these two factors, all the money in China wouldn't be enough to save Mitt's candidacy. What will be interesting to see is after the Bopp experiment has run its course, and the big money fails to win, what will the Congress do about campaign finance reform? To quote the great poet ee cummings:

*"how do you like your blueeyed boy
Mister Death"*

September 20, 2012

Voodoo Two

When candidate George H. W. Bush ran against Ronald Reagan he coined a phrase which became synonymous with the economics policy of the Reagan administration and could easily be applied to Republican orthodoxy since then: "Voodoo Economics."

Bush, the last moderate Republican president, was appalled that Ronald Reagan was proposing to increase federal spending, cut taxes, and balance the budget, a feat that in fact turned out to be impossible. Reagan characterized Jimmy Carter's economic deficits as "obscene" and promised his Presidency was going to erase Carter's deficits and balance the budget.

Bush 41 stated that Reagan's economic views were nonsense and correctly predicted that, if implemented, they would drive up deficits substantially. Calling the Reagan economic proposals, "Voodoo Economics" was his way of alerting the voting public that Reagan's policies were a type of "magical thinking" and had no basis in reality. Just a quick gaze at a chart provided by Wikipedia illustrates the consequence of Reagan's policies on deficits.

In comparison, Carter's deficits look downright puny, although compared to Richard Nixon, they were much larger, leaving Carter vulnerable to the charge that he was increasing the debt more than the frugal Nixon.

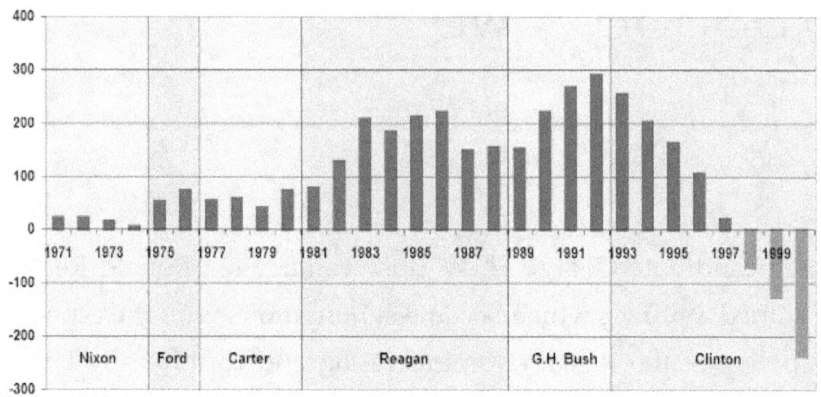

Unfortunately for the nation, Reagan's flirtation with supply side economics led to deficits the likes of which America had never seen before. How and why Ronald Reagan is still considered a hero to conservatives to this day in light of his pursuit of extravagant government spending is beyond my comprehension. The only explanation I can come up with is that in the conservative world, military spending does not count – as by some twisted logic, the Defense Department is not really part of the Federal Government.

Of course, most of us remember that the Soviet Union collapsed during Reagan's term, so he received credit for containment policies dating back to the Truman Administration. If there was one consistent bipartisan thread in American foreign policy since World War II it was an implacable opposition to the Soviet Union. Actually, it was the much maligned Jimmy Carter who stood up to the Soviets the hardest, not with just rhetoric but with bold action. First, he dealt the Soviets a humiliating blow to their collective egos by boycotting the Moscow Olympics, ostensibly for their invasion of Afghanistan. But the most consequential action Carter took was to halt precious shipments of grain to the Soviets, an action that disrupted their food supply chain and led directly to food riots in Poland which marked the beginning of the end of the Soviet empire. But no matter, Reagan uttered those memorable words, "Mr. Gorbachev, tear down this wall!" in Berlin and almost by magic the wall came down. Voodoo indeed.

The Reagan legend was cemented and all the spending was forgiven since Reagan single-highhandedly brought down the despised Soviet empire. Even New York's Mayor Giuliani, running for President himself kept repeating the anecdote that Ronald Reagan had such magical powers that the day he was inaugurated the Iranians released all the hostages from the US Embassy in Teheran. Never mind that the Carter administration had been working feverishly for over a year to negotiate their release, working with as diverse countries as Switzerland and Algeria (the final go-between) to secure the release of the Embassy personnel. No siree, according to the good Mayor of New York City, the mere walking into the White House of the Voodoo Master himself was sufficient to scare the hell out of the Ayatollah, who, out of fear that Reagan might utter magic words like, "Let my people go!" and the hostages would mysteriously disappear from Iran, released them before lunch. It is astounding that there are people who would believe such a fantastical yarn, even devoid of the embellishments I added for effect. Reagan, for the diehard Republicans (and a few Democrats), was the proverbial knight in shining armor and everything he did turned into gold, even when he was selling missiles to the Ayatollah.

Such is the power of magic that Mitt Romney, who in an earlier incarnation put as much distance between himself and Ronald Reagan as he could, has now seen the light and is promoting another version of wizardly wisdom, call it Voodoo Economics 2.0. For brevity sake, let's call it *Voodoo Two*.

Voodoo Two, or the return of Voodoo Economics, is essentially warmed-over Ronald Reagan. If you listen carefully to Mitt Romney (and it is my job to listen carefully to the would-be President) you will get to the essence of what Romney is proposing. He is telling us that he would increase defense spending, lower income taxes for everybody, keep most of the safety net for the poor, save all the entitlements for future generations, and (wait for it) balance the budget. Of course, the main difference between succeeding Obama and succeeding Carter is that between George W. and Obama (mostly George W), the debt has exploded right through the ozone layer. Obama likes to blame Bush for the debt, but he increased the debt by 10% himself, although 90% of it is George W.'s accomplishment.

So Magical Mitt, as we should probably be calling him, together with his wonder-boy Ryan are going to perform a Reagan encore act on an exploding deficit and they expect the American public to believe that Reagan's tripling of Carter's deficit is in no way related to Romney's new voodoo. There are plenty of people who wish to believe. Faith, they call it. But faith in the divine is one thing. Many people believe that faith in the divine is a good thing and who is to say they are wrong? Faith in something we cannot see or comprehend can be construed as optimism, of belief in life with purpose. But confidence in a politician who is doing a bad impersonation of another politician who was responsible for huge deficits is not the kind of faith that can be said to be optimistic. That is just gullibility.

As George W. famously said, "There's an old saying in Tennessee – I know it's in Texas, probably in Tennessee – that says, fool me once, shame on – shame on you. Fool me – you can't get fooled again."

Or something like that.

September 24, 2012

Mitt's Pyrrhic Victory

Most people agree: Mitt won the first debate against the President. The question, therefore is, how did he win it?

He was clearly the aggressor and people generally like their President to be aggressive. Romney correctly figured out that if he was to have a shot at the presidency, he would have to take the fight to the incumbent. Just like in boxing, the challenger has to clearly put the champ on the defensive.

But how did he do it?

In short, he did it by changing his positions one more time, by reinventing himself. If one is keeping track of Romney's positions over his career you could be forgiven if you thought he had multiple personalities. Since Mr. Romney does not have the burden of leading the free world, he is free to change his positions on just about anything to suit his purpose. His hammering away at Obama may have consequences that may not be helpful to the challenger, however. For one, there will be increased scrutiny of Romney's more outlandish claims.

Let's start with the opening of the debate. Romney and Ryan both have been talking about lowering taxes on the "job creators." It is practically Republican gospel that lowering taxes on wealthy people is the path to job creation. George W. did it with disastrous results and, while Obama wants to let the Bush tax cuts die, Romney has indicated that not only does he want to keep the Bush cuts to the very rich, but then lower them even more.

During the initial exchange of last night's debate, however, we learned that no, no, no, the Governor is not about to give any breaks to the rich. His exact words were "I'm not going to reduce the share of taxes paid by high income people." I did a double take so fast that I think I sprained my neck. Later on, in the same segment he said that he wants to bring tax rates down "both for corporations and for individuals." Romney has raised flip-flopping to a new height – he is now flip-flopping within the space of five minutes! He topped his thought when he boldly stated that he would not introduce any tax cut that would "add to the deficit." He doubled down when he reiterated "I will not reduce the taxes paid by high income Americans." Well, that clears it up then. I guess if you have this level of shamelessness, and you don't care about math, it is easier to score debate points.

This is not some small detail in an otherwise great plan. It is the core of Romney's plan, similar to Ronald Reagan's and both Presidents Bushes' plans which gave us astronomical deficits. The older Bush had to actually renege on his "no new taxes" pledge just to prevent the deficits from getting any steeper.

But the whoppers did not end there and we haven't even left the first segment yet. Romney has found a new love for the middle class and wants to lower taxes on them too because he knows that is what people want to hear. And to top it off, he wants to raise defense spending, a cute trick on the way towards his claim of balancing the budget.

In the next segment, when the President repeated his desire to end any tax incentives for companies to ship jobs abroad, Romney played dumb and said he never heard of such a thing in his years in business when his company, Bain Capital took full advantage of that loophole. After many attempts to eliminate the loophole failed in Congress due to Republican opposition it is the height of hypocrisy for Romney to pretend he never heard of this tax break. Again, when you don't have the responsibility of governance, you can make outrageous remarks like this.

On the hot topic of Medicare, after lambasting the President for finding savings in the program, he vaguely alludes to younger recipients that they will be taken care of without specifying how. He is telling young people to just trust him.

On healthcare, Romney elevated hypocrisy to a another level. He finally came across praising his own "Romneycare" which he had been ducking until now and had the gall to say how well it worked in Massachusetts and how "Obamacare," which is based on the Massachusetts model was going to be a disaster for the Nation. He had previously avoided talking about his own healthcare success for fear of being compared to the President's reform. Last night, he threw caution to the wind and just boldly stated that what worked so well in Massachusetts could never serve as a model for the Nation.

When Obama made his case for the federal government having a role in helping education, Romney replied by assuring Americans that he too, supported education, not exactly in the same way as the President, but he too was a believer in teachers, in quality education even though his budget belies his allegations. Obama actually put resources and programs to work to help education, including taking away billions the banks were making at the expense of students seeking college loans. Romney would never have supported that, but claims he is a strong supporter of education. There was no end to the Romney double talk.

One of the truisms Romney uttered last night was that the private marketplace in order to work properly needs rules and regulations. The same applies to debates, one of the ultimate expressions of the free market of ideas. But unlike in boxing, in debates there is no referee. There is nobody taking away points for sucker punches. In boxing, the ref can even disqualify a fighter for fighting dirty. No such things happen in a political debate. There are no rules, no points taken away for low blows, or even for bringing a knife to the fight. Anything goes in politics.

There is an important difference between boxing and debates, however. In boxing the decision is made immediately after the fight and that's all she wrote. In politics winning a debate is more like winning one round. The people are the ones who will ulti-mately decide what the impact of this first round win will be. There will be at least two weeks of poll numbers to judge whether Romney moved the numbers significantly in his direction. Will the celebrated swing states swing in his direction or will they stay with the President, for example. The next debate between the two Presidential candidates will be round two and you can bet that it will go differently depending on where the two stand in the battleground states.

I think Romney may yet regret that he got what he wished for. Winning the first round can produce many unpredictable consequences.

October 4, 2012

Romney's Military-Industrial Complex

"A vital element in keeping the peace is our military establishment. Our arms must be mighty, ready for instant action, so that no potential aggressor may be tempted to risk his own destruction...

This conjunction of an immense military establishment and a large arms industry is new in the American experience. The total influence — economic, political, even spiritual — is felt in every city, every statehouse, every office of the federal government. We recognize the imperative need for this development. Yet we must not fail to comprehend its grave implications. Our toil, resources and livelihood are all involved; so is the very structure of our society. In the councils of government, we must guard against the acquisition of unwarranted influence, whether sought or unsought, by the military-industrial complex. The potential for the disastrous rise of misplaced power exists, and will persist.

We must never let the weight of this combination endanger our liberties or democratic processes. We should take nothing for granted. Only an alert and knowledgeable citizenry can compel the proper meshing of the huge industrial and military machinery of defense with our peaceful methods and goals so that security and liberty may prosper together."

Dwight D. Eisenhower – Farewell to the nation speech, January 16, 1961

In spite of his immense military credentials – or maybe because of them – President Eisenhower warned the nation as he departed the White House of a pernicious trend that portended *"the disastrous rise of misplaced power"* and the need to guard against it.

While most political pundits were bemoaning the head movements of President Obama, the body language of his challenger, and any number of inconsequential facial movements, physical posture, and general demeanor of the two candidates for the most powerful position in the world during their first debate, largely omitted from serious discussion was the President's unchallenged allegation that candidate Romney was proposing a two trillion dollar increase in military spending.

There was more hue and cry over the cutting of Big Bird and the gang at PBS, a savings of approximately $1.25 per average household per year, than the ramping up of our defense establishment to the size of the Cold War years. In those days there was the terrifying thought of nuclear annihilation at the hand of an implacable enemy whose nuclear arsenal was roughly the equivalent to ours and had the wherewithal to deliver a decisive blow that would reduce the United States to ashes in the blink of an eye. Certainly fodder for the hawkish among us.

Nothing approaching this level of Armageddon exists today. The various threats coming from assorted terrorists and potential rogue nations like North Korea and Iran are hardly in the same class of the mighty Soviet Union.

So why, if Mr. Romney is reluctant to borrow a few million from China, as he puts it, to save Big Bird and his pals on Sesame Street, would he be willing to borrow an extra two trillion dollars from presumably the same Chinese? To guard against threats he is not willing to specify? Apparently, children's programming on TV designed to encourage literacy, needs further ample justification but extra trillions for defense only require us to be "concerned." No specifics necessary.

The folks at Foreign Policy magazine have provided us with a chart that illustrates candidate Romney's dream of ramping up defense spending with a historical context dating back to the 1950's, the peak of the Cold War. Please note the smaller spikes for the Korean War and the Vietnam War. The spikes for Iraq and Afghanistan are not on the graph because those wars were not "on the books" as it was an unprincipled trick of the Bush people not to make their reckless spending too obvious.

If most Americans don't get alarmed by this graph, the prospect of a Romney presidency will without a doubt gain the attention of the rest of the world, and not in a good way. America's current enemies will not run and hide, rather they will redouble their efforts, because this is all the proof they need that America would be on a course of world domination. Expect more violence, not less.

As in partial reassurance to our friends and foes alike overseas, let me try to convince you that this is not proof of Romney's desire for world conquest but rather proof of the influence of those who support his campaign.

The infamous *Citizen's United* Supreme court decision, unleash-ing untold secret money to be lavished on our political candid-

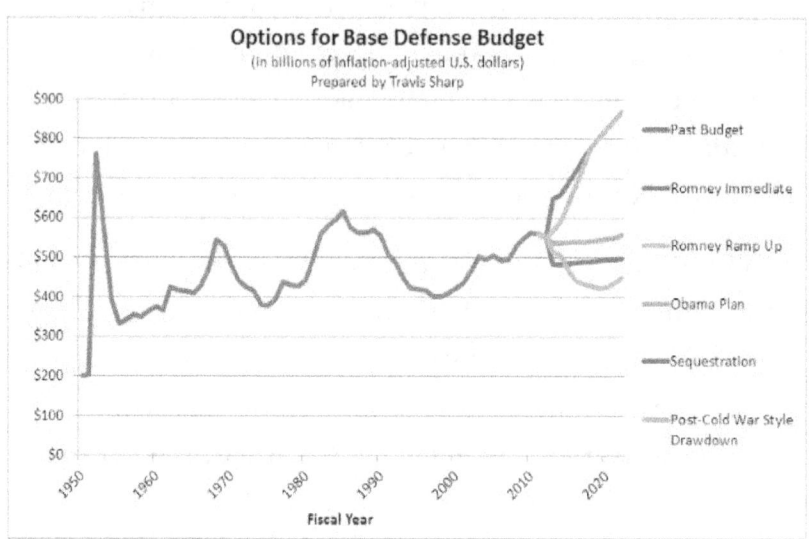

Options for Base Defense Budget
(In billions of Inflation-adjusted U.S. dollars)
Prepared by Travis Sharp

Past Budget
Romney Immediate
Romney Ramp Up
Obama Plan
Sequestration
Post-Cold War Style Drawdown

Fiscal Year

ates, has produced a nightmare scenario that even the astute Dwight Eisenhower could have never predicted. He correctly predicted that there was a kind of vicious circle quality to defense spending by the "Military-Industrial Complex" as he called it. This is a self perpetuating system whereby big defense contractors become reliant on government largesse. Kind of like the welfare queens Republicans like to warn us about. But this is dependency on a massive scale. It is nothing like a poor family relying on food stamps to feed their kids. Rather, it is a mega-empire built on taxpayer funded businesses large, small, and huge depending upon defense contracts to make them profitable. It is government stimulus gone amok.

If Obama had dared spend this kind of money on his stimulus program we would not have any unemployment to speak of and we would indeed be a shining city on a hill. Think Dubai. Yes, the kind of spending proposed by Romney would indeed stimulate the economy. Much employment would be generated, many businesses large and small would thrive, but the country's infrastructure would stay essentially the same. More schools would crumble as would bridges, ports, roads, and so on. We would look fairly good on paper - many people who invested in Romney would get filthy rich - but we would be poorer as a nation because all we would have bought would be a greater capacity to blow up the world many more times over. Overkill on top of more overkill. Not to mention the massive debt we would incur.

I like Big Bird as much as the next guy, but conversation of his survival dwarfs in comparison to the idea of turning this great country of ours into a military nightmare even Eisenhower himself could never have imagined. This is the stuff of dark science fiction movies. Only we're not talking about a movie plot. I have to laugh when I hear folks tell me it makes no difference who gets elected president.

Ralph Nader, are you listening?

October 9, 2012

Joe Scores a KO

It was Joe Biden's night. Those of us who have followed Biden's career knew he had it in him. When paired against the light-weight Palin four years ago they tied one hand behind his back and gave him strict instructions not to manhandle his opponent who had a glaring glass jaw. We have come a long way in gender relations, but there are still many who don't like the sight of a man of the caliber of Joe Biden beating up on a relatively defenseless woman. So fightin' Joe was reduced to a shadow of himself during that bout with the challenged ex-governor of Alaska. It was an awkward moment in American politics.

Last night, no such restrictions were placed on the Vice-President. His opponent this time was the darling of the conservative set – a legitimate intellectual leader of the Republican Party. A man of bold ideas we have been told. President Obama had even said before the 90 minute session that "Joe should be Joe." And Joe he was, warts and all.

It was not all smooth sailing, however. Ryan had a few sucker punches planned much like his running mate had against the President. But unlike the CEO of Bain Capital, Ryan is no closer. In his debate with Obama, the world saw what a first class closer Romney is. You could tell why he was a successful businessman.

It is not hard to imagine, that after the staff at Bain worked painstakingly to explain the intricacies of a complex deal to potential investors the seasoned Romney would appear and put it all together and forcefully close the deal. The great WC Fields summed it up many years ago with his famous quip, "Never give a sucker an even break or smarten up a chump." Romney was not in the business of smartening up anyone. He knew that many of the deals he was promoting were risky, but he knows how to sell iffy to sophisticated investors. That is how he made his living and that is how he beat the intellectually superior Obama. Brawn, when properly applied, can sometimes best brains.

But much as he tried when it was his turn, Ryan was bested from the outset. He did find some weak spots and scored some good blows, but on the important matters he was just outmatched. The murky situation in Libya worked to Ryan's advantage, for example. Being a Monday morning quarterback (if you pardon the mixed metaphor) was relatively easy since the tragic loss of our Ambassador was a result of much confusion on the ground. Romney, in real time, didn't even wait for Monday to commence his second-guessing. He was already pontificating at half-time when we didn't even know what the final score was. It is always unseemly when our people are in harm's way overseas and politicians score cheap political points at their expense. When our soldiers or diplomats are victims of an operation gone wrong, that is not the time to second guess the operation. In the case of the events in Benghazi, considering the intelligence was dicey at best, the prudent (dare I say say conservative) course would have been to stay silent until all the facts were in. But Mitt, always the businessman looking for opportunities, couldn't resist taking advantage of the tragedy to score points against the President. He has been so offensive that the mother of one of the slain Navy SEALS told him to stop using her son as a prop in his campaign. But clever Ryan, with little substance to offer, took the cheap shots against Biden and scored early.

However, when the topics turned to substance and matters of concern to the American voter, Ryan was no match for the well versed Biden, who finally, after waiting four years, could deliver his jabs on substance. On weighty matters such as Medicare, Social Security, the Economy, and the war in Afghanistan, Ryan was taken to school. At one critical point, the Vice-President had to explain the military strategy in Afghanistan to the clueless Ryan, and in the process, educate the American people. Yes, there is a strategy in place, and the reason that fewer American soldiers were engaged was that the Afghan troops we trained were getting more and more involved in securing their own country. And yes, the Taliban are so desperate that they have been able to recruit a few Afghan soldiers to their cause and a few American soldiers tragically lost their lives. Biden correctly pointed out that these were the exceptions, not the rule and the overriding factor was that, imperfect as they are, the Afghans are slowing taking over the responsibility of defending their own country. Unlike the old Soviet Union, America is not out for territorial conquest, just providing a vehicle for the Afghans to create a society where terrorism will have a harder time getting organized to threaten the world.

It is not the intent of this article to go into the whole Vice-Presidential debate blow by blow and document the ups and downs of the clash of the two candidates for the job as a potential Presidential replacement. There will be plenty of commentary examining the details including the equivalent trivial points made about the Presidential debate concerning facial expressions, posture, demeanor and other matters unrelated to governance. I doubt if the American public is that interested in measuring how many seconds Joe Biden smiled, or was that a grin or a smirk on Paul Ryan's face. I leave it to others to discuss these non-issues.

The American voter is more interested in the future of his or her country and whether the teams vying for the privilege to lead this great nation have what it takes to tackle the big issues. On that score the Vice-President showed us all that, unlike Mitt Romney, he won due to his command of the facts and better policies, not due to his superior business closing skills. But he showed us much more. We saw a man whose whole career has been dedicated to defending ordinary Americans. Biden showed us real passion when it came to defending the middle class, seniors, students, women, working people. Ryan, on the other hand was the consummate policy wonk, a cold numbers calculator.

Joe scored the knockout blow when he looked into the camera, referencing Medicare and said "Folks, use your common sense, who do you trust on this? A man who introduced a bill that would raise it sixty-four hundred dollars a year, knowing it, and passing it, and Romney saying he would sign it, or me and the

President?" This statement alone distilled Biden's direct appeal to the Nation. He forcefully illustrated his passion to defend the ordinary citizen. Ryan could only counter with more policy options, more numbers.

Joe Biden showed why in spite of his reputation for speaking off the cuff he has the confidence of the President. Biden did what he had to do. He forcefully defended the interests of most Americans and did it with passion and humor.

President Obama, please take note.

October 12, 2012

The President Gets His Groove Back

Mitt Romney's closing act did not go so well this time around. Mitt was still Mitt, acting up, filibustering, and trying to score points with cheap shots. But this time around the President was determined not to let him get away with anything.

Obama had been roundly criticized after the first debate for letting his opponent "slide," for not engaging him directly, for being too passive and allowing himself to be bullied by the more aggressive Romney. On this blog, I predicted that Romney was going to regret having won his first debate the way he did. ["Mitt's Pyrrhic Victory"] It was clear to me that this time Obama was not going to let Romney get away with what he said without question. Romney succeeded in bringing out the warrior in Obama. The President was nimble, quick and combative. Everything he wasn't in the first debate. What the public saw was their President standing up to a bully. But they also saw their President answering questions from ordinary citizens without evasion.

The President gets a very bad rap about his general demeanor. His calm, deliberative manner gets confused with weakness and

Romney has been quick to exploit this perception. There are many people who don't really understand strength – they confuse strength with bombast, thinking that projecting strength is all about talking "tough." But usually the opposite is true. Leaders who talk "tough" usually do it out of weakness, not strength. Typically, dictators are those who talk the toughest because they live in fear of their own people and need to act tough to intimidate their own populations. The Romney team has built up its whole argument against Obama based on the false premise that our President is weak, that he projects weakness around the world, even that he "leads from behind." That narrative suffered somewhat when Romney was faced with a President who was not going to take a step back from the ever charging Romney, who at times seemed desperate and grasping at straws.

One of the seminal moments of the debate was when Romney, believing in his own propaganda, accused the President of not admitting that the attack on the Benghazi consulate was an act of terror. Obama corrected him and stated calmly that he had said that the very next day in the Rose Garden. Romney doubled down and acted like he had caught the President in a monstrous, lie only to be "fact-checked" on the spot by the rock steady moderator, Candy Crowley, a seasoned reporter from CNN. Obama, seizing the moment even quipped about Candy repeating her correction louder so everyone could hear. Before that, when Romney was committing himself to the proposition that the president was not telling the truth, Obama, sitting on his stool, simply smiled and said, "Please proceed, governor." He was slyly encouraging Romney to hang himself and hang himself he did. Candy Crowley had the presence of mind to correct the record and the video below confirms the truth.[9] It was at this precise moment that Romney's carefully constructed edifice started to crumble. All it takes is one truth teller to point out that the Emperor – in this case the governor – has no clothes.

It never ceases to amaze me in an age when everything is videotaped and it seems everything is available on places like You Tube that any politician would try to falsify a record so easily disproved. And then when caught in a blatant lie, supporters inevitably rally around their candidate and try to tell us that either the record is false or tampered with, or what you can see with your own eyes is not really true.

Finally, as the consummate closer, Romney made a classic mistake. An unforced error. When given the opportunity to correct misconceptions of himself, Romney, who had been caught talking derogatorily about 47% of the American public, tried to overcompensate and said he was for 100% of the people. This gave Obama the opening he was looking for and he didn't miss the opportunity to go into some detail about who the 47% Romney had disparaged were. They were seniors, soldiers, students, even veterans. That Romney, the seasoned politician, businessman and closer extraordinaire, would leave himself open for such a clean punch at the end of a debate calls into question his judgment and his leadership abilities.

October 17, 2012

9   http://www.youtube.com/watch?v=amTUk3rdg1Q

The Closer Versus the Strategist

Mitt Romney spent the better part of this presidential campaign criticizing Barack Obama's foreign policy. He characterized the President as weak, ineffective, and lacking in leadership. But when given the opportunity to debate the President on foreign policy last night he engaged in a surprising amount of "me-too-ism." All of a sudden, with the election on the line, Romney decided to make another one of his now famous flip-flops and found, when given the occasion to show what he would do differently, he chose the more prudent course of agreeing with the President's main foreign policy initiatives. He even went so far as to agree with 2014 as a hard deadline for withdrawing our troops from Afghanistan, a position for which he had previously derided the president for.

By now, nobody should be surprised with the flexible Romney who has pivoted from being a "severe conservative" in order to best his conservative rivals in the Republican primary to being a "moderate" in order to win the presidential election. In Ted Kennedy's immortal words, "I am pro-choice, and Mitt is multiple-choice." That leaves the American public and the entire world, however, in doubt about what would a President Romney in fact do if elected. He has changed positions so many times on so many topics that voters could be excused for being somewhat confused as to what the Republican candidate stands for. For a man who makes a point that the business world needs consistency and certitude in order to conduct business, he has offered us neither.

There was one major point where Romney departed from the President on military policy, however. He made clear once again his desire to spend significantly more money on defense. He is always careful not to say exactly how much more, so as not to scare the average taxpayer already weary about our substantial debt, but the implication is clear, that a massive, Ronald Reagan style military buildup is in store if Romney gets the commander in chief job. There was a point in the debate that was almost comical when he stated that the US Navy had less ships today than before 1917 in an attempt to show that Obama had neglected his defense obligations. The President responded with:

"You mentioned the Navy, for example, and that we have fewer ships than we did in 1916. Well, Governor, we also have fewer horses and bayonets — because the nature of our military's changed. We have these things called aircraft carriers where planes land on them. We have these ships that go underwater, nuclear submarines."

Judging by the laughter in the audience, the President drove home the point that Romney was hopelessly out of touch with how the modern military actually works, that sheer numbers is not what makes our military strong. It is all about capabilities, deployment, and strategy. Obama last night clearly demonstrated his command of military strategy and Romney sounded like a student who had been cramming for an exam.

Even though the President clearly won the foreign policy debate last night, the election will most likely not be won or lost based on foreign policy, which is why Romney ceded the point. He knows he won't best Obama on foreign policy so he is counting on the economy as his strong suit. And that's where it gets interesting.

As pointed out in earlier articles, Romney is a formidable closer. He has made millions convincing skeptical investors to plunk down their millions in business schemes that offered high risk and potential high profitability. He won the first debate hands down exhibiting these closing skills. He lives in the moment and knows how to maximize opportunities. This is how he has run his campaign and it has, by and large, worked if you are inclined to believe the polls. Many people see him as a credible alternative to the cooler, more deliberate Obama who can be frustratingly opaque at times.

When Obama got us involved in the murky war against Muammar Gaddafi, it was not clear what the President was up to. Was he leading? Following? Hence the celebrated phrase "leading from behind." The phrase was not intended as a compliment, but looking back, he got the job done with a fraction of the cost and no American loss of life, unlike the plodding effort in Iraq. As an added bonus, Obama got the French to conduct airstrikes alongside our pilots. Unlike Iraq, the Libya action was a truly allied effort that led to the elimination of a dictator. Best of all, it happened without thousands of American soldiers dead and injured, not to mention another mega-increase in the deficit. This was truly smart power at work. If this is leading from behind then let's have more of it.

Mitt Romney, the consummate business tycoon, is all about quick results – the quarterly report – and in his profession, it is essential. A venture capitalist does not have time to waste on unnecessary items such as developing long term relationships or projecting too far in advance. The turnaround expert is quick to act, get the job done, and walk away as expeditiously as possible. As a matter of fact, expediency is a virtue in Romney's world of business closings.

Governing a complex country with a deeply divided population while dealing with responsibilities all over the world requires patience and lots of it. Romney has shown us time and again that he is not a patient man. He grew tired of governing the infinitesimally smaller territory that is Massachusetts only two years into his governorship. By the time he finished his first and only term he was fed up with governing and allowed Massachusetts to slip to 47th in job creation among our 50 states. His approval rate was in the 30's and he was deemed unelectable for a second term. This is what happens when people are convinced by a quick turnaround artist to govern their state. There is nothing quick about governing. Governing is a marathon, not a sprint. Romney, for example, would make an excellent consultant on a commercial deal with Bolivia, but as CEO of the whole enterprise that is the United States of America he would be a flop, even though he would no doubt shamelessly take advantage of the groundwork prepared by the current President.

Barack Obama, on the other hand is the consummate strategist. He showed us in his primary battle with Hillary Clinton back in 2008. Hillary had all the advantages. She was considered almost the prohibitive favorite and had a hard core of dedicated fans. She had Bill Clinton campaigning for her. Mark Penn, her campaign manager, was one of the best in the business. But unfortunately for her, she was pitted against a real strategist. Obama's supporters kept their hearts in their mouths the whole time, not knowing where Obama was going. He kept things close to the vest much to the consternation of his supporters. He kept everyone in suspense and pulled it out with forward thinking and a superior strategy. The Hillary camp had tactics, Obama had strategy. And if you ask any general worth his or her salt, they will tell you that strategy wins over tactics almost every time.

Barack Obama is one of our first truly strategic Presidents. Richard Nixon was also a strategist but was also a victim of his own self-doubts and paranoia. What is frustrating for many voters, including some of Obama's most ardent supporters, is that there are always questions about what exactly his strategy is. That's all part of the plan since a strategic thinker rarely conveys his strategy, because that is the nature of the master chess player. You are not sure how he does it, but he gets it done with little bombast and fanfare.

It has taken a few years for the Iranian leadership to figure this out. Which is why they are willing to negotiate, albeit in secret. I'm sure the President would love to share what he is doing behind closed doors to bring Iran, kicking and screaming, into dropping their plans for a nuclear weapon, but he can't. That is the nature of power politics. We only get to see the tip of the iceberg. We can only guess what goes on under the surface.

Americans will have a major choice this November. And the choice is not between fake issues like Socialism versus Capitalism. (Hint: both candidates are pro-capitalism.) Or Liberal versus Conservative. (Hint: both candidates are moderates.) No, the choice is more profound and personal.

We have in Mitt Romney, the classic business closer. The king of the deal. The guy you want to convince people to give him their cash and sink it into something they never heard about. Those qualities come in handy at times and it would be an intriguing idea to hire Mitt as a consultant on tangible and complex deals.

We have in Barack Obama, on the other hand, the classic strategic thinker. Calm, cool, and collected. The guy with the steady hand on the tiller of the ship of state. The guy who does not get rattled easily. The guy who is not just thinking short term, but long term as well. The man who will bring this country back slowly, but steadily.

It remains to be seen which quality will prevail among a most volatile electorate.

October 23, 2012

The Next Four Years

One of the few things we can all agree with is that either Barack Obama or Mitt Romney will be elected President next Tuesday. Either we will have a Republican or Democratic House of Representatives and we will have either a Democratic or Republican Senate.

What exactly will happen is anyone's guess as nobody has those kinds of powers of prognostication. But prognosticate we must – not only on the outcome of the election but what it will mean if either of the two principle candidates wins.

The Republicans have invested a lot of time and money telling the American voters that if the President is re-elected expect four years of gridlock and paralysis. Their version of "gloom and doom" is not so much that Barack Obama will do irreparable harm to the country – they also say that – but that the next four years will be wasted as bickering and partisanship will continue unabated, and the important business of the American people will just not get done.

I think they are wrong.

The first Obama term was characterized by a deliberate un-willingness on the part of the Republican leadership to cooperate with the President for the express purpose, in the immortal words of Senate leader Mitch McConnell, "my number one priority is making sure president Obama's a one-term president." The incurably petty will argue whether Mitch said this in 2009 or 2010 (he said it in 2010) but it matters little when he said it since it perfectly illustrates the Senate leader's attitude towards the President. If you examine the record you will see this strategy in action, especially in the Senate, where Mitch McConnell led a record number of filibusters which thwarted majority votes in both Chambers even when the Democrats had the majority in the House of Representatives. This was indeed government by hostage and the intent was clear. Make the President as weak and ineffectual as possible so that come election time the case could be made that he did not deliver on key pieces of legislation, especially important ones like the Jobs Bill. Just the Jobs Bill alone would have made a big dent in our unemployment numbers, but the Republicans were not about to help the economy because that would have practically insured an Obama second term.

If the president wins a second term all of that goes out the window.

Freed from the tyranny of the "one term Presidency" strategy, the Republican Senators could once again vote their conscience and do what they do best: horse-trading and seeking solutions, rather than obstruction for the sake of denying the President a second term. Not that it would spell the end of partisanship or argumentation. That was present during the founding of America and will stay with us as long as there is a Constitutional democracy in the United States. But because the overall obsession of denying Obama a second term will be gone, the Senate will return to a more "normal" state of collegiate belligerence, where both Parties understand the people expect results and co-operation, not continuous obstruction. An Obama second term will be, therefore, full of controversy, but with bipartisan solutions hammered out in vigorous debate. The American people will get a more functional government, spirited, divided, but anxious to find solutions.

So what can we expect from a Romney administration? Regardless of whether the Congress ends up in the hands of the Democrats or the Republicans – it looks like the Republicans will keep a smaller majority in the House, and the Democrats will retain a slim majority in the Senate – the final composition will not matter much. Especially in the Senate where Senator Harry Reid will either stay as a majority or minority leader. Either way will be lethal to a prospective Romney agenda. Senator Reid will become the second most powerful man in the country, second only to the new President himself. Does anybody have a doubt, that after all the humiliation heaped on Senator Reid for the last four years, he will not seek to turn the tables on the Republicans? It is hard to say if the good Senator from Nevada will be more dangerous as the majority or minority leader. There is no plausible scenario that the Republicans will achieve a 60+ majority in the Senate, thereby rendering the Senate filibuster proof. Even the most partisan Republican prognosticator does not contemplate such a dream scenario for the hypothetical President Romney.

So a President Romney would have in Reid an implacable foe who would not hesitate to return the favor of filibustering Republican legislation, if in the minority or just killing it outright if in the majority. In any case, Romney would reap what his party sowed with Obama these last four years and he would have Senator McConnell principally to thank for that. Four years of partisanship and gridlock would face the new President and the merry-go-round would keep turning. This is what happens when shortsighted political expediency is chosen over consensus building governance. And blaming the President for the lack of bi-partisanship is a new height of shamelessness, a new definition for *chutzpah*.

Romney's potential first term has disaster written all over it, and he only has his *compadres* in his own party to blame. On the other hand, if it were not for the high-handed conduct of Republican Senators, making the best of their minority status by denying the President a clear path to governing, Romney would not be neck to neck with the President at this late date. He would be hopelessly behind with no chance of capturing the White House.

So the McConnell strategy did work. Whether the Republicans succeeded at making the President a one term President or not we will find out soon enough.

October 31, 2012

Apocalypse Averted

It turns out that the doomsday predictors were wrong. Even the Mayans are probably wrong.

President Barack Obama was re-elected and the sky didn't fall. Hell did not freeze over. The dollar is still worth basically a dollar. The Dow did not go to zero. Hedge fund managers did not jump out of the windows of their boardrooms. People did not take to the streets *en masse* toting semi-automatic assault rifles.

The President won this election because his appeal was universal. Ironically, the only group that didn't support the President was composed of white men who for some reason still feel threatened by this President. The GOP shamelessly appealed to this group to the exclusion of everyone else and the results showed up on election night. The days when white men dominate this country are over and the GOP needs to recognize that it will not survive as a political force by only appealing to white males and white evangelicals. These two groups have a difficult time recognizing that they are now just two minority groups among so many other minority groups. Unfortunately for the GOP, there are still remnants of hostile, arrogant white males who feel entitled and resent that the rest of the country has a growing piece of the democratic pie. Most baffling of all, is the paranoia among the well-heeled, many of whom act as if they live in a banana republic where the ruler can just arbitrarily confiscate all their wealth.

Exemplifying this latter group is Donald Trump who still acts like the buffoon-in-chief. His antics ranging from his sham run

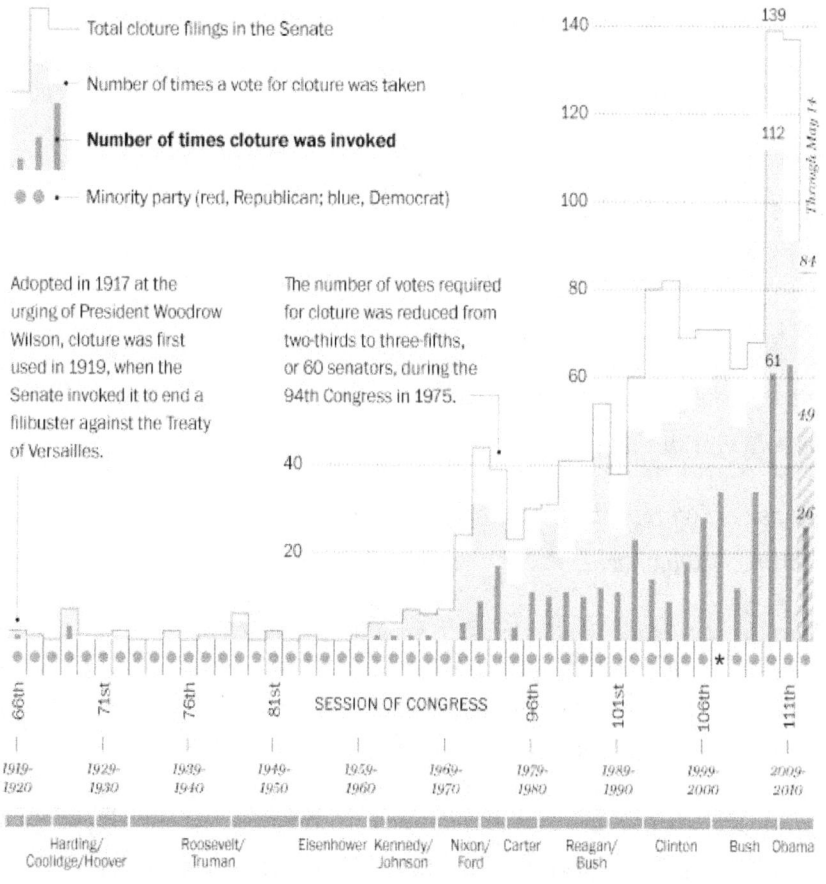

Total cloture filings in the Senate

Number of times a vote for cloture was taken

Number of times cloture was invoked

Minority party (red, Republican; blue, Democrat)

Adopted in 1917 at the urging of President Woodrow Wilson, cloture was first used in 1919, when the Senate invoked it to end a filibuster against the Treaty of Versailles.

The number of votes required for cloture was reduced from two-thirds to three-fifths, or 60 senators, during the 94th Congress in 1975.

SESSION OF CONGRESS

Harding/ Coolidge/Hoover   Roosevelt/ Truman   Eisenhower   Kennedy/ Johnson   Nixon/ Ford   Carter   Reagan/ Bush   Clinton   Bush   Obama

*The minority party of the 107th Congress changed multiple times.

for the presidency to his obsession with the president's birth certificate, college records, and other trivial matters not related to governance would be simply be fodder for comedians if it did not have serious resonance among swaths of the population.

When George W. Bush was President, Trump couldn't have cared less about his college records. But he felt these issues were important when it came to the current President. Trump's narcissism knows no bounds. Here are the comments he tweeted after the announcement of Obama's win:

"This election is a total sham and a travesty. We are not a democracy!"

"More votes equals a loss...revolution!"

"Lets fight like hell and stop this great and disgusting injustice! The world is laughing at us."

"We can't let this happen. We should march on Washington and stop this travesty. Our nation is totally divided!"

"He lost the popular vote by a lot and won the election. We should have a revolution in this country!"

"House of Representatives shouldn't give anything to Obama unless he terminates Obamacare."

"The electoral college is a disaster for a democracy."

"Hopefully the House of Representatives can hold our country together for four more years...stay strong and never give up!"

Donald Trump is an embarrassment to himself, to the Republican Party and to the nation. The bigger point, however, is that the Republican Party has lost credibility when it allows statements of this low caliber to reflect on themselves. If the GOP is to become a relevant political force in the future it has to figure out a way of weeding out this kind of anachronistic thinking. This is not a trivial point. In order for us to succeed as a country we need the adults to take over and work together.

This is a plea for people, all people,

especially politicians, to behave as adults,

and not as spoiled children.

There is no time for infantile antics *à la* the Tea Party. We have already witnessed what happens when the Tea Party Congressmen stamped their feet during the debt ceiling debate with the unfortunate result of our bond rating getting downgraded. For the Nation to succeed we will need the cooperation of both parties. The President has repeatedly indicated that he is willing to work with the opposition. It is really up to the responsible people in the Republican Party to accept this challenge and work constructively with the newly re-elected President.

This is not a plea to muzzle any thoughts. People are free to think as they wish in America. We have a Constitution that guarantees that. This is a plea for people, all people, especially politicians, to behave as adults, and not as spoiled children. The GOP has some serious thinking to do. Do they continue to allow clowns like Trump. Limbaugh and Bachmann to speak for the Party with impunity? At what point does the Republican leadership disavow their messengers of intransigence?

Mitt Romney made a good concession speech in which he exhorted his party to work with the President to solve problems. In Romney's own words, *"The nation, as you know, is at a critical point. At a time like this we can't risk partisan bickering and political posturing. Our leaders have to reach across the aisle to do the people's work, and we citizens also have to rise to the occasion."* The GOP would be wise to follow Romney's advice, not only for their own survival as a Party, but for the sake of a nation that needs more solutions and less chest-thumping.

I predicted on October 31 on this blog [The Next Four Years] that President Obama's second term will be characterized by more bi-partisanship and more consensus building now that the obsession with making the President a one-termer is past. I believe that the American people collectively harbor this hope and that is why they re-elected him. Let's hope we are all right.

November 7, 2012